Preface

ABOUT THE SERIES

THE BEDFORD COLLEGE EDITIONS reprint enduring literary works in a handsome, readable, and affordable format. The text of each work is lightly but helpfully annotated. Prepared by eminent scholars and teachers, the editorial matter in each volume includes a chronology of the life of the author; an illustrated introduction to the contexts and major issues of the text in its time and ours; an annotated bibliography for further reading (contexts, criticism, and Internet resources); and a concise glossary of literary terms. The text of the work is also accessible online at an accompanying Web site (visit *bedfordstmartins .com/americanlit*), where it can be searched electronically.

ABOUT THIS VOLUME

As a supplement to the text of the first American edition of *Charlotte Temple* (1794), the ancillary material in this volume sketches what is known about Susanna Rowson's life as actor, writer, and educator. The introduction provides contexts that will assist readers in developing the historical imagination essential for appreciating a work written more than two centuries ago. It places *Charlotte Temple* in book history as an early best seller, exploring why this novel was popular for so long. It discusses Rowson's philosophy of writing amid the hostility to novel-reading that marked the turn of the nineteenth century. And it engages key questions for responding to the novel in the twenty-first century, questions of genre, identity, authorship, gender, sexuality, family, class, personal autonomy, and community.

ACKNOWLEDGMENTS

I am indebted to two colleagues at Colorado State University whose conversations about this project enriched the introduction. Ruth Alexander (professor of history) and I spent considerable time discussing how early fiction did its cultural work during the Enlightenment. She also steered me to Lynn Hunt's provocative exploration of eighteenth-century epistolary fiction as a catalyst for "inventing human rights." SueEllen Campbell (professor of English) has shared pedagogical strategies that encourage students to ask the kinds of questions that structure the introductory materials here. Since we only find answers to questions we think to ask, she prepares students "to construct nests of questions" and to enjoy rather than reduce the resulting tangles.

Further, I am grateful to Susan Belasco and Linck Johnson, editors of *The Bedford Anthology of American Literature*, for recommending me for this project and for providing useful feedback along the way. Steve Scipione was a supportive press editor, giving clear advice and plenty of space for moving the project to completion. Gloria Blumanhourst gave timely editorial assistance and feedback. Kate Mayhew tied up loose ends and shepherded the manuscript into the production department.

Finally, as always, warm thanks to my partner, Sherry Pomering, whose lively conversation and generosity of spirit contribute more than a few words can acknowledge to every project I undertake.

Pattie Cowell

BEDFORD COLLEGE EDITIONS

Susanna Rowson

Charlotte Temple

Edited by Pattie Cowell
Colorado State University

Bedford/St Martin's
BOSTON • NEW YORK

For Bedford/St. Martin's

SENIOR EXECUTIVE EDITOR: Stephen A. Scipione
EDITORIAL ASSOCIATE: Kate Mayhew
PRODUCTION ASSOCIATE: Samuel Jones
PROJECT MANAGEMENT: Books By Design, Inc.
MARKETING MANAGER: Adrienne Petsick
TEXT DESIGN: Judith Arisman
COVER DESIGN: Donna L. Dennison
COVER ART: Thomas Gainsborough (1727-1788), *Conversation in a Park*, portrait
    of the artist and his wife, Margaret Burr (1728-1798) at the time of their mar-
    riage, 1746. Louvre, Paris, France. Peter Willi/The Bridgeman Art Library.
COMPOSITION: Achorn International, Inc.
PRINTING AND BINDING: RR Donnelley & Sons Company

PRESIDENT: Joan E. Feinberg
EDITORIAL DIRECTOR: Denise B. Wydra
EDITOR IN CHIEF: Karen S. Henry
DIRECTOR OF MARKETING: Karen R. Soeltz
DIRECTOR OF PRODUCTION: Susan W. Brown
ASSOCIATE DIRECTOR OF EDITORIAL PRODUCTION: Elise S. Kaiser
MANAGER, PUBLISHING SERVICES: Emily Berleth

Library of Congress Control Number: 2010928025

Manufactured in the United States of America.

5 4 3
f e d

For information, write: Bedford/St. Martin's,
75 Arlington Street, Boston, MA 02116   (617-399-4000)

ISBN-10: 0-312-59680-4
ISBN-13: 978-0-312-59680-4

Contents

Chronology: The Life of Susanna Rowson

1762   Susanna Haswell born in Portsmouth, England, to William Haswell, Lieutenant in Royal Navy, and Susanna Musgrave Haswell. Mother dies shortly after giving birth.

1763   Left in England with nurse and extended family when navy sends father to Massachusetts. Father settles at Nantasket (now Hull) and in 1765 marries Rachel Woodward.

1766   Brought by father to North America. Survives shipwreck off New England coast.

1775   Placed under house arrest with family at outbreak of American Revolution. Father's property confiscated. Forcibly removed inland to Hingham, Massachusetts.

1777   Haswell family forced to move further inland to Abington, Massachusetts.

1778   Father successfully petitions for family to be sent to Halifax, Nova Scotia. Haswell family later sent to London in prisoner exchange.

1786   Publishes first novel, *Victoria*, by subscription. Marries William Rowson. Begins acting career.

1788   Publishes *A Trip to Parnassus; or, the Judgment of Apollo on Dramatic Authors and Performers*, a comic poem reviewing contemporary London theater. Also publishes her second novel, *The Inquisitor*, and a collection of poems no longer extant.

1789   Publishes third novel, *Mary; or, The Test of Honour*.

1791   Publishes two novels: *Charlotte. A Tale of Truth*, re-titled *Charlotte Temple* in the third American edition, and *Mentoria, or the Young Ladies' Friend*, a multi-genre compilation that functions as a cross between an epistolary novel and a conduct manual.

1792   Publishes sixth novel, *Rebecca; or, The Fille de Chambre*. Pursues acting career in Edinburgh.

1793   Arrives in the United States with husband to join Thomas Wignell's theater company in Philadelphia. Local yellow fever epidemic forces company to move temporarily to Annapolis.

1794   Returns with theater company to Philadelphia. Publishes *Slaves in Algiers*, a play in which she also performs. Publishes first American edition of *Charlotte. A Tale of Truth.*

1795   Publishes seventh novel, *Trials of the Human Heart*, and *The Volunteers*, a play. Attacked for feminism by William Cobbett in *A Kick for a Bite.*

1796   Leaves Philadelphia to join the Federal Street Theater in Boston.

1797   Ends acting career and opens the Young Ladies' Academy in Boston.

1798   Publishes eighth novel, *Reuben and Rachel; or, Tales of Old Times.*

1800   Moves the successful Young Ladies' Academy to a larger home in Medford, Massachusetts.

1802   Contributes essays to the *Boston Weekly Magazine*. Automatically becomes a U.S. citizen when her husband is naturalized.

1803   Moves the Academy to Newton, Massachusetts. Begins serialization of ninth novel, *Sincerity*, in the *Boston Weekly Magazine.*

1804   Publishes *Miscellaneous Poems*, which includes many of Rowson's songs for the theater.

1806   Begins publishing textbooks, the first of which is *An Abridgment of Universal Geography.*

1807   Publishes *A Spelling Dictionary*. Moves the Young Ladies' Academy back to Boston.

1811   Publishes *A Present for Young Ladies*, a compilation of recitations for students that includes several biographies of famous women in history. Moves the Academy to larger quarters in Boston, where it remains for the rest of Rowson's career.

1813   Publishes *Sarah, or The Exemplary Wife*, an epistolary novel lightly reworked from its serialized publication as *Sincerity* a decade earlier.

1817   Contributes essays and songs to the *New England Galaxy*.

1818   Publishes *Youth's First Steps in Geography*.

1822   Retires from the Young Ladies' Academy due to failing health. Publishes *Biblical Dialogues Between a Father and His Family* and *Exercises in History, Chronology and Biography*.

1824   Dies on March 2.

1828   *Charlotte's Daughter; or, The Three Orphans* (later re-titled *Lucy Temple*), a sequel to *Charlotte Temple*, published posthumously.

An Introduction to *Charlotte Temple*

WHEN PHILADELPHIA PUBLISHER Matthew Carey printed the first American edition of *Charlotte Temple* in 1794, he must have been surprised to find he had a best seller on his hands – in fact, the first best seller in America. The print run of 1,000 copies, fairly typical for first editions of late eighteenth-century novels, sold out within a few months. Carey was quick to take advantage. He printed another edition that same year and then added new editions in 1797, 1801, 1802, 1808, 1809, and 1812, not an easy proposition given contemporary book technology, which required hand setting of texts letter by letter, punctuation mark by punctuation mark. In 1801 another Philadelphia publisher as well as publishers from Hartford and New Haven also brought out editions, the first of many outside Philadelphia, making *Charlotte Temple* easily available in several venues, and well on its

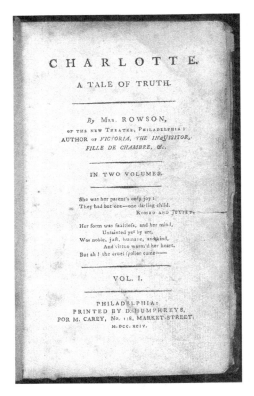

Figure 1. Title page from the first American edition of *Charlotte. A Tale of Truth*, published in 1794 in Philadelphia by Matthew Carey. A surprise best seller, the novel's initial print run of 1,000 copies sold out within a few months. *Clifton Waller Barrett Library of American Literature, Special Collections, University of Virginia Library.*

way to becoming the most popular novel in the United States before *Uncle Tom's Cabin* (1852).[1]

The popularity of the novel brought Susanna Rowson considerable fame, but no royalties. It had already been published in England in 1791 by William Lane of Minerva Press, and Carey simply pirated a copy. Carey's marketing savvy was clear from the beginning. When his edition of *Charlotte Temple* appeared, Rowson was attracting considerable public notice

1. Michael Winship, "Two Early American Bestsellers: Rowson's *Charlotte Temple* and Stowe's *Uncle Tom's Cabin*," *Common-Place* 9.3 (April 2009), n. pag. Web. 7 September 2009. <www .common-place.org>.

as part of a local acting company. Carey reminded potential book buyers of this fact on the title page, noting that Rowson was "of the New Theatre, Philadelphia." He went on to establish her credibility as a writer by listing the titles of her three previous novels. Further sweetening his bottom line, Carey had no obligation to share the proceeds of his sales with Rowson. Her English book could not be copyrighted in the United States because it was not until 1891 that the U.S. began to recognize international copyrights.

More than two hundred editions later,[2] *Charlotte Temple* is a success story that should not be ignored, and this introduction to yet another edition outlines why Rowson's simple tale of seduction and villainy still finds readers.

SUSANNA ROWSON'S LIFE AND TIMES[3]

Though Susanna Rowson wrote a fair number of autobiographical fictions, *Charlotte Temple* is not among them. It would be hard to describe an author less like her most famous protagonist. Rowson was purposeful in shaping her life and her life story; Charlotte Temple reacted to people and events as they came to her. Rowson reinvented herself as needs and circumstances required; the teenage Charlotte had no chance to learn that she had choices and that they mattered. At a time when most middle-class white women were caught in the daily demands of domesticity, Rowson forged a public role for herself as writer, actor, and educator; in contrast, the fictional Charlotte Temple followed the conventional eighteenth-century script for "fallen" women.

Unlike Charlotte, Susanna Rowson was wise enough to understand the power of social and literary convention and strong enough to use them rather than be used by them. She knew the script, but she had other stories in mind for herself and most of her fictional creations. Born Susanna Haswell in 1762 in Portsmouth, England, Rowson was named after her mother, Susanna Musgrave Haswell, who died soon after giving birth. Her father, British Royal Navy Lieutenant William Haswell, was posted to Massachusetts

2. Cathy N. Davidson, "Ideology and Genre: The Rise of the Novel in America," *Proceedings of the American Antiquarian Society* 96 (1986): 298. Print; reprinted with slight revisions as "The Life and Times of *Charlotte Temple*: The Biography of a Book," in *Reading in America: Literature & Social History,* ed. Cathy N. Davidson (Baltimore: Johns Hopkins UP, 1989), 157-79. Print.
3. Much of the factual basis for reconstructing Rowson's life is drawn from the research of Patricia L. Parker, published in *Susanna Rowson* (Boston: Twayne, 1986), especially chapter 1, and "Susanna Rowson," *American Women Prose Writers to 1820*, ed. Carla Mulford with Angela Vietto and Amy E. Winans (Detroit: Gale, 1999), 313-25. Print.

in 1763 as a collector of Royal customs, and he left his small daughter with relatives until 1766, when he brought her to Nantasket (now Hull), Massachusetts, to join him and his new wife, Rachel Woodward. It was a difficult Atlantic crossing, and Rowson's recollections of that first voyage turn up years later in her fiction. There is no record of schooling, but Susanna had access to her father's small library, where she had the opportunity to read literary works by William Shakespeare and Edmund Spenser, translations such as Dryden's *Virgil* and Pope's *Homer*, and the writings of philosopher David Hume. Perhaps she had access to the circulating library in Nantasket. Rowson recalled these childhood years as happy ones, filled with connections to a host of educated family friends, among them the well-known patriot James Otis, who called her his "little pupil."

The dislocations of the Revolutionary War soon put an end to this comfortable middle-class routine. William Haswell tried to maintain his neutrality. He had lived in Massachusetts for twelve years. His wife and sons were North American–born. He owned property in Massachusetts and knew it would be forfeited if he actively supported the king. But as a member of the British Navy living on the strategically important Nantasket Peninsula, he aroused the suspicion even of former friends. The war came to them, as Boston was occupied by the British and provisioned through Nantasket Harbor. One of several nearby skirmishes ended with a British retreat through Haswell's property. Rowson recalls in one of her later autobiographical fictions that the officer in charge left a dying soldier with the Haswells, and Susanna helped her father bury him in their backyard. Neutrality was no longer an option. His property confiscated, William Haswell was moved with his family inland to Hingham, in effect interned away from coastal locations of potential military value and forced to live on an allowance that wasn't sufficient for family needs. By 1777, 15-year-old Susanna found herself with her family further inland in Abington, caring for ailing and depressed parents, two small half brothers, and her step-grandmother. It was winter when they arrived. Their house was small, with dirt floors and windows that let in wind and snow. Susanna gathered wood, cooked over an open fire, and with the help of friends, kept the family fed and sheltered until they were granted permission by the General Court of Massachusetts to travel to Halifax, Nova Scotia, where they became part of a prisoner exchange. By the end of 1778 the Haswells were back in London, destitute among hundreds of other refugees from the former colonies. Rowson later remembered the kindness of patriot friends who made their war-time survival possible, thanking them in the preface to her aptly titled novel *Trials of the Human Heart* (1795).

Figure 2. Portrait of Susanna Rowson as a young woman. *Papers of Susanna Rowson. Clifton Waller Barrett Library of American Literature, Special Collections, University of Virginia Library.*

It took months, perhaps years, for the Haswells to understand that they would not be returning to their home and work in Massachusetts, and longer still for William Haswell's restitution and retirement claims to be settled. They passed their time as best they could, frequenting the less-expensive entertainments of London, visiting parks, sightseeing, and most important for Susanna, going to the theater, perhaps at Drury Lane or Covent Garden. Because her parents' illnesses continued and her half brothers were too young to help, Susanna became the financial mainstay for the family. Records detailing her early efforts are scarce, but an autobiographical passage from one of her novels suggests she might have been a teacher or a governess. During this period, she began writing song lyrics, some of them for Vauxhall Gardens, a London venue for entertainment much like a present-day theme park. By 1786, when her father's finances improved sufficiently to support his family, Susanna had cultivated a patron, Georgiana Cavendish, Duchess of Devonshire, who helped to obtain subscribers to finance the publication of her first novel, *Victoria.*

Figure 3. Pencil sketch of a young William Rowson, c. 1770. *Papers of Susanna Rowson.*
Clifton Waller Barrett Library of American Literature, Special Collections, University of Virginia Library.

In 1786 Susanna Haswell married William Rowson, a less-than-successful actor, musician, and hardware merchant. Once again, Rowson found herself the financial anchor for her family, equal to the task but not happy with it, and as the years went by, not particularly happy with William either. He was unable to keep a job, had a knack for running up debt more quickly than Susanna could pay it off, and in later years drank heavily. During Rowson's life and throughout much of the nineteenth century, both England and the United States enforced the legal concept of coverture, under which a married woman's rights to property and person were merged into those of her husband. Though Susanna was the chief Rowson breadwinner, William controlled their finances. Despite the friction this legal and personal situation created, they remained together, and though they had no children, they raised his illegitimate son, adopted two daughters, supported William's younger sister when his parents died, and later supported her children as well. Several biographers have remarked that the epigraph on the title page of one of Rowson's later novels, *Sarah, or The Exemplary Wife* (1813), might be read as a commentary on her situa-

Figure 4. Engraving by M. Marigot of Philadelphia's Chestnut Street Theatre (initially deemed the New Theatre), where Susanna Rowson performed after she and husband William left England. *Free Library of Philadelphia.*

tion: "Do not marry a fool; he is continually doing absurd and disagreeable things, for no other reason but to shew he dares do them."[4]

Early in their marriage, Susanna and William shared careers as actors, though Susanna had considerably more success than William, particularly as a comedian. Mostly they performed in towns outside London, including Edinburgh, though at least once Susanna made a London appearance. During her years on the English stage, Rowson continued writing, publishing fiction, poetry, a pamphlet about the London theater, and an "Essay on Female Education." In 1791 William Lane of Minerva Press published the first edition of her fourth novel, *Charlotte. A Tale of Truth* (re-titled *Charlotte Temple* in the third American edition). Though it received a favorable review and was to bring Rowson considerable fame in the United States, it received little attention in England.

4. The epigraph is taken from Scottish writer John Gregory, who wrote *A Father's Legacy to His Daughters,* a conduct book for women much reprinted in the late eighteenth and early nineteenth centuries.

SUSANNA HASWELL ROWSON
From a miniature still owned in the family

Figure 5. Portrait of Susanna Rowson. *From Rowson,* Charlotte Temple: A Tale of Truth, *ed. Francis W. Halsey (New York, 1905). Clifton Waller Barrett Library of American Literature, Special Collections, University of Virginia Library.*

By 1793, Susanna and William realized they could not make a living on the English stage and accepted an offer from actor and theater entrepreneur Thomas Wignell to join an American acting company. As Matthew Carey was bringing out the first American edition of *Charlotte Temple* in 1794, Susanna Rowson was performing at Philadelphia's New Theatre in a series of challenging roles, including a part in a play she had written herself, *Slaves in Algiers; or, a Struggle for Freedom.* She handled thirty-five roles in her first Philadelphia season, enjoyed recognition from the brisk sales of *Charlotte Temple,* witnessed the publication of American editions of three other books previously published in England, and continued to write songs for the theater. Fearing that Wignell's theater venture was in financial trouble, Susanna and William Rowson joined the Federal Street Theater company in Boston in 1796. Susanna appeared in some forty different productions there, but by the end of the 1797 season, the Federal Street Theater faced bankruptcy, and Rowson made a career change.

She opened Mrs. Rowson's Young Ladies' Academy and ran the school in several locations in and near Boston with much success until she retired

Figure 6. Portrait of William Rowson. By J. R. Smith, 1819. *Papers of Susanna Rowson. Clifton Waller Barrett Library of American Literature, Special Collections, University of Virginia Library.*

in 1822. Within a year she had more than one hundred students, many of them from prominent families, and others on a waiting list. The academy allowed Rowson to pursue her lifelong commitment to women's and girls' education more comprehensively than she had been able to in her writing. Her curriculum adapted ideas from progressive theorists of female education, combining a conventional program of study for middle-class white girls – practical skills in domestic economy, music, painting, dancing, embroidery, French – with science, geography, mathematics, composition, history, and biography. She used classroom materials that included accounts of women in history and in other cultures. When she couldn't find appropriate texts, she wrote them herself. In 1805, for example, she published *An Abridgment of Universal Geography*, which included remarks on women in various Asian countries. In 1811 she published *A Present for Young Ladies*, an anthology of recitations she had written for students to present at annual public exhibitions. Most of the pieces highlight educated, accomplished, self-confident women as role models.

Susanna Rowson died in 1824, after a career spanning more than forty years as actor, lyricist, novelist, playwright, poet, essayist, teacher, and educational businesswoman. Writing and teaching were essential to her financial well-being and that of her family, but they were also motivated by a lifelong sense of civic responsibility. Rowson saw herself and other writers as entertainers, but more importantly as educators, as carriers of cultural values that would, or at least should, concern readers. In her preface to *Trials of the Human Heart* (1795), she assures readers that "it has ever been my pride, that I never yet wrote a line that might tend to mislead the untutored judgment, or corrupt the inexperienced heart; and heaven forbid I should suffer ought to escape my pen, that might call a blush to the cheek of innocence, or deserve a glance of displeasure from the eye of the most rigid moralist."[5]

Not everyone saw her work as quite so safe. Critics and commentators in the eighteenth and early nineteenth centuries often treated the increasing popularity of fiction with suspicion or outright hostility. Some found novels, including Rowson's, dangerous, particularly for women readers. In 1803, Samuel Miller, a Presbyterian minister and later a faculty member at Princeton Theological Seminary, captured the substance of much of this criticism:

> All classes of persons in society, from the dignified professional character to the lowest grades of laboring indigence, seek and devour novels. . . . Every opportunity is taken [in novels] to attack some principle of morality . . . ; to ridicule the duties of domestic life . . . ; to deny the sober pursuits of upright industry . . . ; and, in a word, to frame an apology for suicide, adultery, prostitution, and the indulgence of every propensity for which a corrupt heart can plead an inclination. . . . The author has no hesitation in saying, that, if it were *possible*, he would *wholly* prohibit the reading of novels. . . . For it may, with confidence, be pronounced that NO ONE WAS EVER AN EXTENSIVE AND ESPECIALLY AN HABITUAL READER OF NOVELS, EVEN SUPPOSING THEM ALL TO BE WELL SELECTED, WITHOUT SUFFERING BOTH INTELLECTUAL AND MORAL INJURY, AND OF COURSE INCURRING A DIMINUTION OF HAPPINESS.[6]

5. [Susanna] Rowson, *Trials of the Human Heart* (Philadelphia: Wrigley & Berriman for Rice, 1795), 4 volumes, I, xv. Print. Subsequent references to this novel are included parenthetically in the text.
6. Samuel Miller, *A Brief Retrospect of the Eighteenth Century* (New York: T. and J. Swords, 1803), 2 volumes, II, 172, 175, 179. Print. Capital letters and italics in original.

Miller was not alone in his concern that novels undermined what seemed to him to be stable community morals. Nor was he the only writer to charge that individual readers of novels were harmed by their reading experience. Such reading was for Miller at best a waste of time, but worse than that, suggestible readers (those from "the lowest grades of laboring indigence") might be led astray, their values compromised, their behavior injurious to themselves and others.

This may sound a bit hysterical to twenty-first-century readers who accept fiction as a staple among their reading choices. But at the turn of the nineteenth century, leaders accustomed to setting community norms and articulating what they promoted as shared values found their authority eroding. The population was increasingly literate. Individuals had more venues for information and entertainment than ever before. New printing technologies and distribution networks made books, magazines, and newspapers more accessible and cheaper. For those for whom books were still not cheap enough, circulating libraries proliferated, featuring novels as an important part of their collections. Reading was becoming a private act, unmediated by church or state. Knowledge as a form of power was becoming increasingly diffuse. What was to restrain individuals if novels incited them to licentious behavior? Who would speak for virtue and family if novels tempted readers to follow their "inclinations"? Though he collected and read novels himself, Thomas Jefferson warned that they were dangerous for women and the poor. John Adams and Noah Webster were also among those public figures who assailed the novel.

Women were considered to be particularly at risk from novel reading, since they had less access to education, and fiction was thought to undermine their allegedly weaker judgment. An anonymous poet in the *American Magazine, or General Repository* advised female readers that they should protect themselves from unhealthy influences and ambitions: "Seek to be good, but aim not to be great / A woman's noblest station is retreat...."[7] Even education theorists cautioned that women's instruction should only be pursued "to every prudent length" for fear of impairing their "more tender health."[8] Physician and writer Benjamin Rush spoke at the Young Ladies' Academy in 1787, the same year in which he published

7. "Advice to a Young Lady," *The American Magazine, or General Repository* (July, 1769): 224; reprinted as "Advice to the Ladies," *Virginia Gazette*, ed. Purdie and Dixon (May 16, 1771), [4]. Print.
8. James Fordyce, "On Female Virtue, with Intellectual Accomplishments," in *Sermons to Young Women* ([Boston: Mein and Fleeming], 1767), 11, 15. Print.

his well-regarded *Thoughts upon Female Education*. He argued that an appropriate and widespread program of women's education would benefit not only women but the entire community, especially as they assumed their roles as wives and mothers. But the flip side of the proposition was also true for Rush. A misguided education, one that instilled "that passion for reading novels, which so generally prevails among the fair sex," could lead to social disruption. Novels promoted a consciousness that "blunts the heart to that which is real." He didn't exempt Rowson's fiction from his charge: "we sometimes see instances of young ladies, who weep away a whole forenoon over the criminal sorrows of a fictitious Charlotte or Werter."[9]

Rush wasn't the only prominent critic of Rowson's fiction. English pamphleteer and journalist William Cobbett, writing under the pseudonym Peter Porcupine, savaged Rowson in *A Kick for a Bite* (1795). He was particularly incensed by feminist themes in Rowson's play *Slaves in Algiers*, and quotes at length from passages such as this one questioning patriarchal gender expectations: "woman was never formed to be the abject slave of man. Nature made us equal with them, and gave us the power to render ourselves superior." Arguing that such ideas undermine custom, Cobbett sarcastically predicted that reformers will "raze the odious word *obey* from their marriage service." He devoted so much of his vituperation to *Slaves in Algiers* that when he moved on to Rowson's novels, he had space for only a few scathing remarks on their effects as emetics and opiates.[10]

After Cobbett's attack, several commentators rushed to Rowson's aid, perhaps unnecessarily. No stranger to the frank and often blistering directness of late eighteenth-century critics, Rowson used the preface to *Trials of the Human Heart* (1795) to respond: "I find myself obliged to remark that the literary world is infested with a kind of loathsome reptile, . . . for it cannot be ranked with propriety amongst either authors or critics," one of which [read Cobbett] "has lately crawled over the volumes, which I have had the temerity to submit to the public eye. I say *crawled over* them, because I am certain it has never penetrated beyond the title-page of any" (xiii–xiv). Rowson's comfort in such exchanges was probably enhanced by her knowledge that even negative reviews attracted attention and readers to her work. The already established popularity of her novels was a kind of defense in itself. There must have been considerable satisfaction in knowing that her readers far outnumbered Cobbett's.

9. Benjamin Rush, *Thoughts upon Female Education* (Boston: Samuel Hall, 1787), 11–12. Print. "Werter" is likely drawn from Goethe's *The Sorrows of Young Werther* (1774).
10. William Cobbett, *A Kick for a Bite* (Philadelphia: Thomas Bradford, 1795), 23, 24, 27. Print.

CHARLOTTE TEMPLE AND NEW NOTIONS OF SELFHOOD[11]

Much like early commentators who worried about the power of fiction to unravel the social fabric, more recent readers of *Charlotte Temple* and other early novels have remarked that the act of reading fiction has consequences that go beyond the purely aesthetic. They recognize the importance of questions about form and technique, about how a writer achieves the effects she does, questions such as why Rowson chose to use an intrusive narrator in *Charlotte Temple* or the extent to which the scenic structure of the novel was influenced by Rowson's experience on the stage. But they also note that by themselves such questions of form cannot explain why *Charlotte Temple* has been read, enjoyed, attacked, and analyzed by so many for so long. By themselves such explorations do not address the ways in which *Charlotte Temple* and other forms of popular literature have been both agent and product of social change.

For that we must turn to broader questions: How is it significant that the development of the novel in the eighteenth century coincided with new understandings of selfhood, individualism, and democracy? What made novels so popular and their readers so diverse? What did it mean to be an author at the turn of the nineteenth century? How did that differ from authorial identity earlier in the eighteenth century? What concepts and practices relating to gender, sexuality, marriage, and family were developing during this period in America? How do we account for the fact that most of the novels written in the new United States advocated greater access to education for women and the poor?

Responses to questions like these remind us that ideas and practices we sometimes take for granted — self, democracy, sexuality, marriage — change over time. Consider, for example, the concept of authorship, which was undergoing profound change during Rowson's life. Early in the eighteenth century, an author or writer was viewed as a craftsman, one who understood the rules of rhetoric and poetics and used that understanding to pass along inherited wisdom using traditional forms. By the time Rowson began writing, a new concept of authorship was working alongside the old, one in which authors were seen to work from inspiration. Rather than taking their forms and messages from external authorities, they drew their materials from within. The inspired writer created original works,

11. Ideas developed here are much indebted to historian Lynn Hunt, *Inventing Human Rights* (New York: Norton, 2007), whose first chapter, "'Torrents of Emotion': Reading Novels and Imagining Equality," explores eighteenth-century European epistolary novels as embodiments of new modes of human relationship.

which became what we now call intellectual property. To encourage this inspired writing, nations began to consider the appropriateness of copyright laws. By the early nineteenth century U.S. writers such as Washington Irving and James Fenimore Cooper were able to support themselves solely from their publications. Although Rowson could not support herself entirely with her prolific writing, it nevertheless became a significant part of her financial well-being and identity.

Changing notions of authorship contributed to the development of fiction as a new literary genre. Scholars of Europe and North America have remarked on the surge in popularity of the novel in the eighteenth century. In France, eight new novels were published in 1701, fifty-two in 1750, and 112 in 1789. The numbers are even more dramatic in Britain. Between 1700 and 1760 there was a sixfold increase in new novels published. About thirty new novels appeared annually in the 1770s, forty in the 1780s, and seventy in the 1790s.[12] There were no indigenous novels in America before the Revolution. The colonists read fiction, but it was either directly imported from abroad or pirated by American printers who faced no constraints from international copyright laws. For a variety of reasons — the first national copyright in 1790, the popularity of the new genre, changing technologies of printing — U.S. writers were drawn to this new form late in the eighteenth century. Between 1789 and 1820 roughly one hundred American novels were published.[13]

These books were called "novel" for a reason. They were new in both form and content. Their storytelling format and character development made them readable without advanced education in the classics. Newly affordable and widely available, novels were read by servants as well as masters, women as well as men, and people in both urban and rural communities. Evidence drawn from extant lending-library rosters, subscription lists published in novels, booksellers' records, and inscriptions found in extant copies of novels points to the wide economic, social, and geographic diversity of readers.[14]

Furthermore, unlike earlier literature featuring kings, gods, and superheroes, the narrative content of most novels centered on middle- and working-class people, men and women in life situations much like those

---

12. Hunt, *Inventing Human Rights*, 40.

13. Cathy N. Davidson, *Revolution and the Word: The Rise of the Novel in America* (New York: Oxford UP, 1986), viii, 11. Print. An expanded edition appeared in 2004, but page numbers here are drawn from the 1986 edition unless otherwise noted.

14. Marian Rust, *Prodigal Daughters: Susanna Rowson's Early American Women* (Chapel Hill: U of North Carolina P, 2008), 77-81, 133. See also Davidson, *Revolution and the Word*, expanded edition, 29-30. Print.

of readers, facing questions of economic security, work, love, marriage, family, faith, values, and relationships. Eighteenth-century novels were studies in the workings of character, in both senses of the word. As readers saw elements of themselves in a wide range of fictional characters, they had an opportunity to experience selves that were separate from their stations. They observed that characters were formed of gender, class, ethnicity, and nation, but that they were also more than the sum of these parts. Imaginative identification allowed readers to practice alternative selves. Their reading contributed to a growing sense of personal autonomy as they were presented with new frameworks for selfhood embodied in fiction. They were attracted by something like Immanuel Kant's sense that humans reach a new level of maturity when they develop a "determination and courage to use [their] intelligence without being guided by another," a turning away from traditional sources of authority and toward the self.[15]

These may seem like strange claims for a novel whose central character lacks autonomy from beginning to end. Living away from her parents at a boarding school, Charlotte ricochets from one authority figure to another. She is swayed by one of her teachers, Mademoiselle La Rue, and by her seducer Montraville. She fails to grasp what is happening when Belcour sets a scene that conveniently persuades Montraville she has been unfaithful to him. She is taken under the protective wing of Mrs. Beauchamp, who then is absent at the crucial moments of Charlotte's last crisis, when she allows herself to be driven into a snowstorm by her unnamed American landlady. Charlotte is so lacking in agency that one recent critic pointedly asks, "What's wrong with Charlotte Temple?" and another builds much of her analysis on images of Charlotte as childlike.[16]

But the novel *Charlotte Temple* is not coterminous with the character Charlotte Temple. Rowson informs readers in her brief preface that she wants her novel of be "of service" to those "who are so unfortunate as to have neither friends to advise, or understanding to direct them" (37).[17] She puts the novel (and not incidentally, herself) in the role of another kind of authority, one who teaches by example rather than by dictate.

15. Immanuel Kant, "What Is Enlightenment?" [1784], in *The Philosophy of Kant*, ed. Carl J. Friedrich (New York: Modern Library, 1949), 132-39. Print.

16. Marian Rust, "What's Wrong with *Charlotte Temple?*" *William and Mary Quarterly*, third series, 60.1 (January 2003): 99-118. Print. A revised version of the essay is included in Rust's *Prodigal Daughters*, 48-103. Ann Douglas provides an extended analysis of Charlotte Temple's childlike qualities in her introduction to *Charlotte Temple and Lucy Temple* (New York: Penguin, 1991), vii-xliii. Print.

17. All page references to *Charlotte Temple* are to this edition and are inserted parenthetically in the text.

Figure 7. Engraving of Rowson's Charlotte Temple, created by C. Tiebout in 1812. By this point, the book had been printed by publishers in cities beyond Philadelphia, rendering it easily accessible in a variety of venues and poised to become the most popular novel in the United States at the time. *Papers of Susanna Rowson. Clifton Waller Barrett Library of American Literature, Special Collections, University of Virginia Library.*

Significantly, the single extended subplot in *Charlotte Temple*, the story of Charlotte's parents and maternal grandparents, provides a countervailing example to Charlotte. If Charlotte is unclear about what she values for her future, if she is undone by adolescent "inclination" and naïveté, her parents' story is different. They make difficult choices and live with the consequences. Charlotte's father, Henry Temple, defies his father, the Earl of D —, to marry Lucy Eldridge, an impoverished woman whom he loves, rather than Miss Weatherby, his father's choice, a woman described by the narrator as uncultivated, unfeeling, impetuous, given to dissipation, and rich. Henry loses his inheritance and his father but gains life with the partner of his choice.

Rowson's novel suggests that Henry Temple's bargain is a good one, both in outcome and process. The late eighteenth-century world in which her fictional characters live placed high value on an individual's freedom to make meaningful choices and to assume direct responsibility for one-self. The absolute authority of fathers over children had eroded. Marriage choices were increasingly in the hands of partners rather than parents. Romantic love rather than economic security or advantage became a key motivation for marriage.[18] Religious authority had been weakened by changing demographics and new attitudes toward democracy. American revolutionaries had declared that "all men are created equal" and that they "are endowed by their Creator with certain unalienable Rights." If the nation's early leaders did not quite mean it, if "all men" with choices were only those white males with property, they had nevertheless unleashed a "rights talk" they would not be able to contain.

But such a rights talk played out differently for groups of individuals in the new United States. If Henry Temple's bargain is a good one for him, it turns out to be disastrous for his daughter. She doesn't so much defy her parents, of course, as ignore them. But for her, the consequences are severe.

Enlightenment ideas about the value of the individual, the desirability of autonomy, and the importance of choice are significant precisely because they are more than ideas. They are also practices which can only enter a novel or a legal system embodied. The sex of the body, its color, its citizenship (or lack of citizenship), and its class turn out to matter in ways that abstract rights talk didn't mention. Henry Temple could make choices his daughter could not.

Bound into the first American edition of *Charlotte Temple* (1794) was an advertisement for Mary Wollstonecraft's *A Vindication of the Rights of Woman* (1792), a document that questioned revolutionary ideology by inaugurating a new kind of rights talk. Published a year after the first English edition of *Charlotte Temple*, Wollstonecraft's *Vindication* asks readers to think about distinctions between rights for men and for women. Why were men's rights the political rights of citizens and women's rights synonymous with the duties of wife and mother? Why did rights have gender? Wollstonecraft used this rights talk for relatively modest ends. Rather than advocating for rights similar to those of men, she made a case for stronger and more accessible education for girls and increased professional opportunities for women. Wollstonecraft argued that education

18. Jan Lewis, "The Republican Wife: Virtue and Seduction in the Early Republic," *William and Mary Quarterly*, third series, 44 (October 1987): 689-721. Print. See also Jay Fliegelman, *Prodigals and Pilgrims: The American Revolution Against Patriarchal Authority, 1750-1800* (Cambridge: Cambridge UP, 1982). Print.

would give girls and women the rational foundation for making effective life choices, for self-cultivation, and for meeting their responsibilities to others. She argued that better-educated women would build stronger families and communities, in effect benefiting men as well as women.[19]

Though Rowson's politics were considerably more conservative than Wollstonecraft's, she shared Wollstonecraft's concern for female education. Rowson intended her fiction, however entertaining or provocative the hook, to be as didactic as the classrooms she presided over in the last twenty-five years of her career. And like Wollstonecraft, she intended her writing to open avenues to a more autonomous selfhood for deserving (read white and middle-class) women. Story was her tool, but not subtlety. *Charlotte Temple*'s narrator made sure readers were following the lessons as well as the plot. The narrator is bold and confident enough to interrupt the story several times with a direct address to readers containing homilies for young and old, male and female. Some of these messages reinforce explicitly the less direct message of Henry Temple's story. They warn young female readers that "it is now past the days of romance: no woman can be run away with contrary to her own inclination" (55). Having chosen their actions, characters and readers alike must live with the consequences.

CHARLOTTE TEMPLE AND COMMUNITY

As conservative eighteenth-century leaders were quick to point out, increased individualism, personal autonomy, and the erosion of cultural traditions created danger as well as opportunity in the new American republic. Founding documents proclaimed a new national unity, but what was to balance the atomizing force of separate selves, unregulated and uncontained by social institutions? What was to prevent Thomas Hobbes's seventeenth-century prediction that individual lives in a state of nature would be "nasty, brutish, and short" from becoming a self-fulfilling prophecy? Were there ways in which novels like *Charlotte Temple* and other forms of popular literature could help individuals make connections across potentially divisive personal differences of ethnicity, race, gender, class, region, religion, and language? Could novelists like Rowson exploit the fact that readers used to mixing instruction with entertainment didn't draw firm distinctions between fiction and nonfiction? How

---

19. For a more detailed discussion of late eighteenth-century rights talk, see Rosemarie Zagarri, "The Rights of Man and Woman in Post-Revolutionary America," *William and Mary Quarterly*, third series, 55.2 (April 1998): 203–30. Print.

might the popularity of eighteenth-century sentimentalism, in its appeal to affect or emotion, give fiction a role in building relationships beyond family and kinship networks and faith communities? How might fiction have a role in nation-building?

To untangle questions like these, it helps to remember that the strong impetus toward order and community-building in the eighteenth century was in part a response to seventeenth-century philosophers like Hobbes. Eighteenth-century leaders as diverse as Benjamin Franklin, Thomas Jefferson, Judith Sargent Murray, and John Adams understood that the cultivation of the self was most easily provided for in community. New notions of personal autonomy were not in conflict with strong communities because selves were created in relationship rather than in isolation.

Fiction provided a tool for trying on new relationships and their consequences. Novels functioned as mirrors, reflecting the struggles, aspirations, and temptations of readers, providing imaginative practice for real-life encounters. They encouraged readers to project themselves into characters' situations, to imagine relationships they had had no experience with, and to understand that others' experiences of selfhood might parallel their own. As historian Lynn Hunt phrased it, fiction became "a kind of hothouse of emotional learning."[20] Readers cultivated a growing set of perceptions about what people are like, what they value, how they negotiate right and wrong in an increasingly secular environment, and how they move in a world that distributes power unequally. In settings close to home, novels provided situations and characters that touched readers' interior, emotional lives.

The eighteenth-century term to describe this imaginative identification process was *sympathy*. Though sympathy is now more often used to describe a feeling of pity or sadness at the distress of others, in the eighteenth century it conveyed an affective understanding of one's shared humanity. An individual used his or her capacity for sympathy to relate to the experiences of others, even others one might not know. At a time when new notions of selfhood functioned to separate people, sympathy provided a countervailing force. It created human bonds that formed the bedrock of community, a personal basis for civic engagement.

Rowson shared an understanding of the power of sympathy[21] with her readers, and exploited its positive valence again and again in *Charlotte*

---

20. Hunt, *Inventing Human Rights*, 55.
21. It is no accident that the first American novel is titled *The Power of Sympathy*. Written by William Hill Brown, it was published in 1789.

Temple. One example early in the novel is worth quoting at length for illustration. This example features a conversation between Charlotte's father, Henry, and her grandfather, Captain Eldridge, long before Charlotte is born. Note that the workings of sympathy, of emotion and affect, were as powerful for eighteenth-century men as for women. In this scene, Henry listens to Captain Eldridge explain how he had been cheated out of his fortune, sent to debtor's prison, and had lost his wife and son as a result. Eldridge chokes up as he speaks and is embarrassed at losing his composure. Henry is quick to comment:

> . . . "the truly brave soul is tremblingly alive to the feelings of humanity."
>
> "True," replied the old man, (something like satisfaction darting across his features) "and painful as these feelings are, I would not exchange them for that torpor which the stoic mistakes for philosophy. How many exquisite delights should I have passed by unnoticed, but for these keen sensations, this quick sense of happiness or misery? . . ."
>
> "This is true philosophy," said Temple. [45]

Later in their extended exchange, Henry urges Captain Eldridge to "keep up your spirits . . . ."

> "You never lost a wife and son," said Eldridge.
>
> "No," replied [Henry], "but I can feel for those that have." [48]

Both men value the cultivation of emotional understanding, first for its intrinsic value to oneself and then as a connective link in relationship. Henry has not yet lost his daughter; in fact, he doesn't yet have a daughter. But his sympathy for the straitened circumstances of Captain Eldridge allows him to "feel for those that have." Eldridge's experience foreshadows Henry's, and Henry's sympathy is part of his emotional preparation for later loss. Sympathy forms a pathway to communication and understanding across differences in age and experience, the beginnings of what Benedict Anderson has called "imagined communities." Deriving from novels and other forms of popular literature, such "imagined communities" create some of the glue that holds real communities and nations together.[22]

---

22. Benedict Anderson, *Imagined Communities: Reflections on the Origin and Spread of Nationalism*, Revised edition (1983; London: Verso, 2006), 24–36. Print.

As a sentimental novel, *Charlotte Temple* gives form to the eighteenth-century value expressed as sympathy. Accustomed to understating even intense emotions, twenty-first-century readers sometimes wince at what they take to be overly mannered or excessive expressions of feeling. But in the eighteenth and early nineteenth centuries, the sentimental novel was a revolutionary form confronting issues of authority, class privilege, gender, personal autonomy, intimacy, and interpersonal moral obligation. It explored the relationship between domestic life and society, private and public spaces. It asked readers to consider which circumstances would allow individuals to achieve their potential and which would stunt

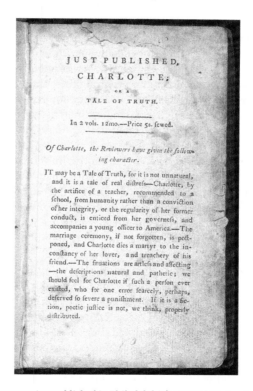

Figure 8. Anonymous review published in Philadelphia's *Critical Review* in 1794. By this point in the eighteenth century, novels had become quite popular, generating immense interest as well as harsh critical scrutiny. While readers were drawn to the entertainment value inherent in the novel's fictional reality, critics feared they threatened community morals. *From Rowson,* Charlotte. A Tale of Truth *(Philadelphia, 1794). Clifton Waller Barrett Library of American Literature, Special Collections, University of Virginia Library.*

personal growth. It questioned (and sometimes reinforced) conventional relationships between men and women, parents and children, masters and servants. In its efforts to encourage good conduct, it risked asking what we mean by "good."

Much influenced by such novelists as Samuel Richardson (England), Laurence Sterne (Ireland), and Henry Mackenzie (Scotland), sentimental fiction was a staple of reading fare in the new United States. In addition to imports from Europe, recently established magazines such as *Boston Magazine, American Museum,* and *New York Magazine* published a steady stream of sentimental short stories. By the 1790s, American writers such as Charles Brockden Brown, Hannah Foster, William Hill Brown, and Tabitha Tenney were adding an American flavor to the genre.

Sentimental novels typically combined an emphasis on emotional expression with a concern for ethical behavior. Plots involving courtship and seduction were common, and stock characters abound – dictatorial fathers forcing daughters and sons to marry against their will, wily young men of privilege looking for sexual conquests, innocent young working women or naïve middle-class girls, virtuous and trustworthy male heroes. Judgments of character are one-dimensional, without shades of gray, often creating an element of melodrama. Those who behave inappropriately end up remorseful or dead. Rowson uses this sentimental formula to interesting effect. The seducer Montraville ends up with a bad case of melancholy, though by all outward trappings his story should have a "happy-ever-after" ending. The other villains die in carefully described misery.

But the novel's conclusions about morality are more complex than the melodramatic formulas of sentimental fiction imply. For all its narrative simplicity, *Charlotte Temple* addresses issues of civic as well as personal morality, and the social system is found wanting. Charlotte's naïveté and inappropriate education lead her to make foolish choices, but behind those choices is a system of female dependence that limits her ability to take care of herself. Deprived of citizenship, of the legal and economic tools requisite to selfhood, labeled a "fallen" woman, she is vulnerable. In direct addresses to readers, Rowson's narrator models expressions of sympathy. She urges them to "feel the woes of Charlotte" (109) and to identify with her by "reflect[ing] how many errors we are ourselves subject to, how many secret faults lie hid in the recesses of our hearts, which we should blush to have brought into open day" (85). In effect, the narrator judges the social system rather than Charlotte, because it has deprived her of necessary tools for selfhood: knowledge of the world and agency. Because the social system is on trial here and not Charlotte, unrealized ideals of selfhood and democracy are exposed as measures of collective rather than individual failing.

As sentimental fiction grew in popularity, so did its critique, frequently coming out as parody of over-the-top emotional expression, floods of tears and frequent fainting. English novelist Henry Fielding, for example, published *Shamela* (1741) within months of the publication of Samuel Richardson's sentimental hit *Pamela* (1740). Rowson was as aware of the parodies as she was of the popularity of the sentimental formula. Her narrator imagines a "young, volatile reader" exclaiming "'I shall never have patience to get through these volumes, there are so many ahs! and ohs! so much fainting, tears, and distress, I am sick to death of the subject'" (109). But Rowson is convinced enough of the power of sympathy to devote most of a chapter to persuading readers to persist and to cultivate their consciences until they are able to empathize with Charlotte. She reminds these skeptical readers that she is writing "a tale of truth" and she means "to write it to the heart" (109).

The "truth" of her tale is important enough to Rowson to merit repeated reference. She calls *Charlotte Temple* a "tale of truth" in the subtitle, the preface, and the novel itself. She claims to have heard the story from "an old lady who had personally known Charlotte" and to "have thrown over the whole a slight veil of fiction" (37). Sentimental readers took her at her word. They were more than eager to blur the boundaries between fiction and nonfiction. They speculated on which historical individuals Charlotte and Montraville stand in for. And for most of a century, tens of thousands of them made pilgrimages to a grave purported to be Charlotte Temple's in New York City's Trinity Churchyard, leaving flowers, locks of hair, and a variety of personal mementos. No one knows who, if anyone, is actually buried there because parish records were twice destroyed by fires, or who initially associated the grave with the fictional Charlotte. But during the nineteenth century, Charlotte's grave was one of the most popular draws in Trinity Churchyard. It continues to attract the curious even today.[23]

What are twenty-first-century readers to make of a best seller that became an American icon or a fictional character embalmed in nineteenth-century imaginations? How are we to understand that a novel written in England by an English woman and first published in London functioned for more than a hundred years as part of the cultural glue connecting a

23. Lisa M. Gordis, "'None Need Think Their Sympathy Wasted,'" *Common-Place* 9.3 (April 2009). n. pag. Web. 7 September 2009. <www.common-place.org>.

Figure 9. Charlotte Temple's gravestone in New York City's Trinity Churchyard. It is un-clear whether anyone is actually buried there, as parish files were destroyed by fires, but visitors continue to frequent the site, leaving flowers or personal keepsakes. *From Rowson,* Charlotte Temple: A Tale of Truth, *ed. Francis W. Halsey (New York, 1905). Clifton Waller Barrett Library of American Literature, Special Collections, University of Virginia Library.*

new American nation? If we think of American books as those published in the United States, written by American writers, featuring American set-tings about American characters (or at least some of the above), *Charlotte Temple* doesn't seem to qualify. But by now these become rhetorical ques-tions. *Charlotte Temple* figures strongly in early American literature cur-ricula and scarcely if at all in English literary canons.

Once again, Rowson asks readers to examine their categories and question their premises. She felt at home in the United States, but she never claimed an American identity. She praised the new nation, wrote patriotic songs and poems, and expressed gratitude to the friends who helped her family survive the revolution. She didn't become a U.S. citi-zen until her husband became naturalized in 1802. Like so many outsider observers – Crèvecoeur and de Tocqueville come to mind – she implicitly asked whether identity is more complicated than point of origin, for books as well as for people. Cathy Davidson made a strong case that *Charlotte Temple* was read as an American book, marketed as an American book, and naturalized into an American cultural icon for most of the nineteenth century.[24] She suggested that *Charlotte Temple* may not be the same novel after its transatlantic crossing. However complex its identity, somewhere on the journey it took on a fascination it hasn't lost.

24. Davidson, "Life and Times of *Charlotte Temple*," 158, 165-171.

A Note on the Text

The text printed here is from the first American edition, published by Matthew Carey as *Charlotte. A Tale of Truth* (Philadelphia, 1794). The title *Charlotte Temple*, used by Carey in the third American edition (Philadelphia, 1797), is the one most frequently chosen for subsequent editions.

Eighteenth-century spelling and grammar have been retained throughout, though the long "∫" has been changed to an "s." A few obvious typographical errors have been silently corrected: a wrongly numbered chapter, missing quotation marks, broken or missing font, and the like.

Charlotte Temple

Susanna Rowson

CONTENTS

[VOLUME II]

Preface

FOR THE PERUSAL of the young and thoughtless of the fair sex, this Tale of Truth is designed; and I could wish my fair readers to consider it as not merely the effusion of Fancy, but as a reality. The circumstances on which I have founded this novel were related to me some little time since by an old lady who had personally known Charlotte, though she concealed the real names of the characters, and likewise the place where the unfortunate scenes were acted: yet as it was impossible to offer a relation to the public in such an imperfect state, I have thrown over the whole a slight veil of fiction, and substituted names and places according to my own fancy. The principal characters in this little tale are now consigned to the silent tomb: it can therefore hurt the feelings of no one; and may, I flatter myself, be of service to some who are so unfortunate as to have neither friends to advise, or understanding to direct them, through the various and unexpected evils that attend a young and unprotected woman in her first entrance into life.

While the tear of compassion still trembled in my eye for the fate of the unhappy Charlotte, I may have children of my own, said I, to whom this recital may be of use, and if to your own children, said Benevolence, why not to the many daughters of Misfortune who, deprived of natural friends, or spoilt by a mistaken education, are thrown on an unfeeling world without the least power to defend themselves from the snares not only of the other sex, but from the more dangerous arts of the profligate of their own.

Sensible as I am that a novel writer, at a time when such a variety of works are ushered into the world under that name, stands but a poor chance for fame in the annals of literature, but conscious that I wrote with a mind anxious for the happiness of that sex whose morals and conduct have so powerful an influence on mankind in general; and convinced that I have not wrote a line that conveys a wrong idea to the head or a corrupt wish to the heart, I shall rest satisfied in the purity of my own intentions, and if I merit not applause, I feel that I dread not censure.

If the following tale should save one hapless fair one from the errors which ruined poor Charlotte, or rescue from impending misery the heart of one anxious parent, I shall feel a much higher gratification in reflecting on this trifling performance, than could possibly result from the applause which might attend the most elegant finished piece of literature whose tendency might deprave the heart or mislead the understanding.

Chapter I.

A Boarding School

"ARE YOU FOR A WALK," said Montraville to his companion, as they arose from table; "are you for a walk? or shall we order the chaise and proceed to Portsmouth?" Belcour preferred the former; and they sauntered out to view the town, and to make remarks on the inhabitants, as they returned from church.

Montraville was a Lieutenant in the army: Belcour was his brother officer: they had been to take leave of their friends previous to their departure for America, and were now returning to Portsmouth, where the troops waited orders for embarkation. They had stopped at Chichester to dine; and knowing they had sufficient time to reach the place of destination before dark, and yet allow them a walk, had resolved, it being Sunday afternoon, to take a survey of the Chichester ladies as they returned from their devotions.

They had gratified their curiosity, and were preparing to return to the inn without honouring any of the belles with particular notice, when Madame Du Pont, at the head of her school, descended from the church. Such an assemblage of youth and innocence naturally attracted the young soldiers: they stopped; and, as the little cavalcade passed, almost involuntarily pulled off their hats. A tall, elegant girl looked at Montraville and blushed: he instantly recollected the features of Charlotte Temple, whom he had once seen and danced with at a ball at Portsmouth. At that time he thought on her only as a very lovely child, she being then only thirteen; but the improvement two years had made in her person, and the blush of recollection which suffused her cheeks as she passed, awakened in his bosom new and pleasing ideas. Vanity led him to think that pleasure at again beholding him might have occasioned the emotion he had witnessed, and the same vanity led him to wish to see her again.

"She is the sweetest girl in the world," said he, as he entered the inn. Belcour stared. "Did you not notice her?" continued Montraville: "she had on a blue bonnet, and with a pair of lovely eyes of the same colour, has contrived to make me feel devilish odd about the heart."

"Pho," said Belcour, "a musket ball from our friends, the Americans, may in less than two months make you feel worse."

"I never think of the future," replied Montraville; "but am determined to make the most of the present, and would willingly compound with any kind Familiar who would inform me who the girl is, and how I might be likely to obtain an interview."

But no kind Familiar at that time appearing, and the chaise which they had ordered, driving up to the door, Montraville and his companion were obliged to take leave of Chichester and its fair inhabitant, and proceed on their journey.

But Charlotte had made too great an impression on his mind to be easily eradicated: having therefore spent three whole days in thinking on her and in endeavouring to form some plan for seeing her, he determined to set off for Chichester, and trust to chance either to favour or frustrate his designs. Arriving at the verge of the town, he dismounted, and sending the servant forward with the horses, proceeded toward the place, where, in the midst of an extensive pleasure ground, stood the mansion which contained the lovely Charlotte Temple. Montraville leaned on a broken gate, and looked earnestly at the house. The wall which surrounded it was high, and perhaps the Argus's who guarded the Hesperian fruit within, were more watchful than those famed of old.[1]

" 'Tis a romantic attempt," said he; "and should I even succeed in seeing and conversing with her, it can be productive of no good: I must of necessity leave England in a few days, and probably may never return; why then should I endeavour to engage the affections of this lovely girl, only to

---

1. *Argus*: In Greek mythology, Argus is a hundred-eyed giant set to guard Io, priestess of Hera, the goddess of women and marriage. Distracted and killed by Hermes, he fails in his task. The Hesperides were nymphs charged with tending a tree of golden apples that had been given by Gaia to Hera when she married Zeus. Since the Hesperides occasionally picked an apple, Hera set the dragon Ladon to guard the tree. Ladon also fails as a guardian when he is killed by Heracles, who then steals the apples.

leave her a prey to a thousand inquietudes, of which at present she has no idea? I will return to Portsmouth and think no more about her."

The evening now was closed; a serene stillness reigned; and the chaste Queen of Night with her silver crescent faintly illuminated the hemisphere. The mind of Montraville was hushed into composure by the serenity of the surrounding objects. "I will think on her no more," said he, and turned with an intention to leave the place; but as he turned, he saw the gate which led to the pleasure grounds open, and two women come out, who walked arm-in-arm across the field.

"I will at least see who these are," said he. He overtook them, and giving them the compliments of the evening, begged leave to see them into the more frequented parts of the town: but how was he delighted, when, waiting for an answer, he discovered, under the concealment of a large bonnet, the face of Charlotte Temple.

He soon found means to ingratiate himself with her companion, who was a French teacher at the school, and, at parting, slipped a letter he had purposely written, into Charlotte's hand, and five guineas into that of Mademoiselle, who promised she would endeavour to bring her young charge into the field again the next evening.

Chapter II.

Domestic Concerns

MR. TEMPLE was the youngest son of a nobleman whose fortune was by no means adequate to the antiquity, grandeur, and I may add, pride of the family. He saw his elder brother made completely wretched by marrying a disagreeable woman, whose fortune helped to prop the sinking dignity of the house; and he beheld his sisters legally prostituted to old, decrepid men, whose titles gave them consequence in the eyes of the world, and whose affluence rendered them splendidly miserable. "I will not sacrifice internal happiness for outward shew," said he: "I will seek Content; and, if I find her in a cottage, will embrace her with as much cordiality as I should if seated on a throne."

Mr. Temple possessed a small estate of about five hundred pounds a year; and with that he resolved to preserve independence, to marry where the feelings of his heart should direct him, and to confine his expenses within the limits of his income. He had a heart open to every generous feeling of humanity, and a hand ready to dispense to those who wanted part of the blessings he enjoyed himself.

As he was universally known to be the friend of the unfortunate, his advice and bounty was frequently solicited; nor was it seldom that he sought out indigent merit, and raised it from obscurity, confining his own expenses within a very narrow compass.

"You are a benevolent fellow," said a young officer to him one day; "and I have a great mind to give you a fine subject to exercise the goodness of your heart upon."

"You cannot oblige me more," said Temple, "than to point out any way by which I can be serviceable to my fellow creatures."

"Come along then," said the young man, "we will go and visit a man who is not in so good a lodging as he deserves; and, were it not that he has an angel with him, who comforts and supports him, he must long since have sunk under his misfortunes." The young man's heart was too full to proceed; and Temple, unwilling to irritate his feelings by making further enquiries, followed him in silence, til they arrived at the Fleet prison.

The officer enquired for Captain Eldridge: a person led them up several pair of dirty stairs, and pointing to a door which led to a miserable, small apartment, said that was the Captain's room, and retired.

The officer, whose name was Blakeney, tapped at the door, and was bid to enter by a voice melodiously soft. He opened the door, and discovered to Temple a scene which rivetted him to the spot with astonishment.

The apartment, though small, and bearing strong marks of poverty, was neat in the extreme. In an arm-chair, his head reclined upon his hand, his eyes fixed on a book which lay open before him, sat an aged man in a Lieutenant's uniform, which, though threadbare, would sooner call a blush of shame into the face of those who could neglect real merit, than cause the hectic of confusion to glow on the cheeks of him who wore it.

Beside him sat a lovely creature busied in painting a fan mount. She was fair as the lily, but sorrow had nipped the rose in her cheek before it was half blown. Her eyes were blue; and her hair, which was light brown, was slightly confined under a plain muslin cap, tied round with a black ribbon; a white linen gown and plain lawn handkerchief composed the remainder of her dress; and in this simple attire, she was more irresistibly charming to such a heart as Temple's, than she would have been, if adorned with all the splendor of a courtly belle.

When they entered, the old man arose from his seat, and shaking Blakeney by the hand with great cordiality, offered Temple his chair; and there being but three in the room, seated himself on the side of his little bed with evident composure.

"This is a strange place," said he to Temple, "to receive visitors of distinction in; but we must fit our feelings to our station. While I am not ashamed to own the cause which brought me here, why should I blush at my situation? Our misfortunes are not our faults; and were it not for that poor girl – "

Here the philosopher was lost in the father. He rose hastily from his seat, and walking toward the window, wiped off a tear which he was afraid would tarnish the cheek of a sailor.

Temple cast his eye on Miss Eldridge: a pellucid drop had stolen from her eyes, and fallen upon a rose she was painting. It blotted and discoloured the flower. " 'Tis emblematic," said he mentally: "the rose of youth and health soon fades when watered by the tear of affliction."

"My friend Blakeney," said he, addressing the old man, "told me I could be of service to you: be so kind then, dear Sir, as to point out some way in which I can relieve the anxiety of your heart and increase the pleasures of my own."

"My good young man," said Eldridge, "you know not what you offer. While deprived of my liberty I cannot be free from anxiety on my own account; but that is a trifling concern; my anxious thoughts extend to one more dear a thousand times than life: I am a poor weak old man, and must expect in a few years to sink into silence and oblivion; but when I am gone, who will protect that fair bud of innocence from the blasts of adversity, or from the cruel hand of insult and dishonour."

"Oh, my father!" cried Miss Eldridge, tenderly taking his hand, "be not anxious on that account; for daily are my prayers offered to heaven that our lives may terminate at the same instant, and one grave receive us both; for why should I live when deprived of my only friend."

Temple was moved even to tears. "You will both live many years," said he, "and I hope see much happiness. Cheerly, my friend, cheerly; these passing clouds of adversity will serve only to make the sunshine of prosperity more pleasing. But we are losing time: you might ere this have told me who were your creditors, what were their demands, and other particulars necessary to your liberation."

"My story is short," said Mr. Eldridge, "but there are some particulars which will wring my heart barely to remember; yet to one whose offers of friendship appear so open and disinterested, I will relate every circumstance that led to my present, painful situation. But my child," continued he, addressing his daughter, "let me prevail on you to take this opportunity, while my friends are with me, to enjoy the benefit of air and exercise. Go, my love; leave me now; to-morrow at your usual hour I will expect you."

Miss Eldridge impressed on his cheek the kiss of filial affection, and obeyed.

Chapter III.

Unexpected Misfortunes

"MY LIFE," said Mr. Eldridge, "till within these few years was marked by no particular circumstance deserving notice. I early embraced the life of a sailor, and have served my King with unremitted ardour for many years. At the age of twenty-five I married an amiable woman; one son, and the girl who just now left us, were the fruits of our union. My boy had genius and spirit. I straitened my little income to give him a liberal education, but the rapid progress he made in his studies amply compensated for the inconvenience. At the academy where he received his education he commenced an acquaintance with a Mr. Lewis, a young man of affluent fortune: as they grew up their intimacy ripened into friendship, and they became almost inseparable companions.

"George chose the profession of a soldier. I had neither friends or money to procure him a commission, and had wished him to embrace a nautical life: but this was repugnant to his wishes, and I ceased to urge him on the subject.

"The friendship subsisting between Lewis and my son was of such a nature as gave him free access to our family; and so specious was his manner that we hesitated not to state to him all our little difficulties in regard to George's future views. He listened to us with attention, and offered to advance any sum necessary for his first setting out.

"I embraced the offer, and gave him my note for the payment of it, but he would not suffer me to mention any stipulated time, as he said I might do it whenever most convenient to myself. About this time my dear Lucy returned from school, and I soon began to imagine Lewis looked at her with eyes of affection. I gave my child a caution to beware of him, and to look on her mother as her friend. She was unaffectedly artless; and when, as I suspected, Lewis made professions of love, she confided in her parents, and assured us her heart was perfectly unbiassed in his favour, and she would chearfully submit to our direction.

"I took an early opportunity of questioning him concerning his intentions towards my child: he gave an equivocal answer, and I forbade him the house.

"The next day he sent and demanded payment of his money. It was not in my power to comply with the demand. I requested three days to endeavour to raise it, determining in that time to mortgage my half pay, and live on a small annuity which my wife possessed, rather than be under an obligation to so worthless a man: but this short time was not allowed me; for that evening, as I was sitting down to supper, unsuspicious of danger, an officer entered, and tore me from the embraces of my family.

"My wife had been for some time in a declining state of health: ruin at once so unexpected and inevitable was a stroke she was not prepared to bear, and I saw her faint into the arms of our servant, as I left my own habitation for the comfortless walls of a prison. My poor Lucy, distracted with her fears for us both, sunk on the floor and endeavoured to detain me by her feeble efforts; but in vain; they forced open her arms; she shrieked, and fell prostrate. But pardon me. The horrors of that night unman me. I cannot proceed."

He rose from his seat, and walked several times across the room: at length, attaining more composure, he cried – "What a mere infant I am! Why, Sir, I never felt thus in the day of battle."

"No," said Temple; "but the truly brave soul is tremblingly alive to the feelings of humanity."

"True," replied the old man, (something like satisfaction darting across his features) "and painful as these feelings are, I would not exchange them for that torpor which the stoic mistakes for philosophy. How many exquisite delights should I have passed by unnoticed, but for these keen sensations, this quick sense of happiness or misery? Then let us, my friend, take the cup of life as it is presented to us, tempered by the hand of a wise Providence; be thankful for the good, be patient under the evil, and presume not to enquire why the latter predominates."

"This is true philosophy," said Temple.

" 'Tis the only way to reconcile ourselves to the cross events of life," replied he. "But I forget myself. I will not longer intrude on your patience, but proceed in my melancholy tale.

"The very evening that I was taken to prison, my son arrived from Ireland, where he had been some time with his regiment. From the distracted expressions of his mother and sister, he learnt by whom I had been arrested; and, late as it was, flew on the wings of wounded affection, to the house of his false friend, and earnestly enquired the cause of this cruel conduct. With all the calmness of a cool deliberate villain, he avowed his passion for Lucy; declared her situation in life would not permit him to marry her; but offered to release me immediately, and make any settlement on her, if George would persuade her to live, as he impiously termed it, a life of honour.

"Fired at the insult offered to a man and a soldier, my boy struck the villain, and a challenge ensued. He then went to a coffee-house in the neighbourhood and wrote a long affectionate letter to me, blaming himself severely for having introduced Lewis into the family, or permitted him to confer an obligation, which had brought inevitable ruin on us all. He begged me, whatever might be the event of the ensuing morning, not to suffer regret or unavailing sorrow for his fate, to encrease the anguish of my heart, which he greatly feared was already insupportable.

"This letter was delivered to me early in the morning. It would be vain to attempt describing my feelings on the perusal of it; suffice it to say, that a merciful Providence interposed, and I was for three weeks insensible to miseries almost beyond the strength of human nature to support.

"A fever and strong delirium seized me, and my life was despaired of. At length, nature, overpowered with fatigue, gave way to the salutary power of rest, and a quiet slumber of some hours restored me to reason, though the extreme weakness of my frame prevented my feeling my distress so acutely as I otherways should.

"The first object that struck me on awaking, was Lucy sitting by my bedside; her pale countenance and sable dress prevented my enquiries for poor George: for the letter I had received from him, was the first thing that occurred to my memory. By degrees the rest returned: I recollected being arrested, but could no ways account for being in this apartment, whither they had conveyed me during my illness.

"I was so weak as to be almost unable to speak. I pressed Lucy's hand, and looked earnestly round the apartment in search of another dear object.

"Where is your mother?" said I, faintly.

"The poor girl could not answer: she shook her head in expressive silence; and throwing herself on the bed, folded her arms about me, and burst into tears.

"What! both gone?" said I.

"Both," she replied, endeavouring to restrain her emotions: "but they are happy, no doubt."

Here Mr. Eldridge paused: the recollection of the scene was too painful to permit him to proceed.

Chapter IV.

Change of Fortune

"IT WAS SOME DAYS," continued Mr. Eldridge, recovering himself, "before I could venture to enquire the particulars of what had happened during my illness: at length I assumed courage to ask my dear girl how long her mother and brother had been dead: she told me, that the morning after my arrest, George came home early to enquire after his mother's health, staid with them but a few minutes, seemed greatly agitated at parting, but gave them strict charge to keep up their spirits, and hope every thing would turn out for the best. In about two hours after, as they were sitting at breakfast, and endeavouring to strike out some plan to attain my liberty, they heard a loud rap at the door, which Lucy running to open, she met the bleeding body of her brother, borne in by two men who had lifted him from a litter, on which they had brought him from the place where he fought. Her poor mother, weakened by illness and the struggles of the preceding night, was not able to support this shock; gasping for breath, her looks wild and haggard, she reached the apartment where they had carried her dying son. She knelt by the bed side; and taking his cold hand, 'my poor boy,' said she, 'I will not be parted from thee: husband! son! both at once lost. Father of mercies, spare me!' She fell into a strong convulsion, and expired in about two hours. In the mean time, a surgeon had dressed George's wounds; but they were in such a situation as to bar the smallest hopes of recovery. He never was sensible from the time he was brought home, and died that evening in the arms of his sister.

"Late as it was when this event took place, my affectionate Lucy insisted on coming to me. 'What must he feel,' said she, 'at our apparent neglect, and how shall I inform him of the afflictions with which it has pleased heaven to visit us?'

"She left the care of the dear departed ones to some neighbours who had kindly come in to comfort and assist her; and on entering the house where I was confined, found me in the situation I have mentioned.

"How she supported herself in these trying moments, I know not:

heaven, no doubt, was with her; and her anxiety to preserve the life of one parent in some measure abated her affliction for the loss of the other.

"My circumstances were greatly embarrassed, my acquaintance few, and those few utterly unable to assist me. When my wife and son were committed to their kindred earth, my creditors seized my house and furniture, which not being sufficient to discharge all their demands, detainers were lodged against me. No friend stepped forward to my relief; from the grave of her mother, my beloved Lucy followed an almost dying father to this melancholy place.

"Here we have been nearly a year and a half. My half-pay I have given up to satisfy my creditors, and my child supports me by her industry: sometimes by fine needlework, sometimes by painting. She leaves me every night, and goes to a lodging near the bridge; but returns in the morning, to chear me with her smiles, and bless me by her duteous affection. A lady once offered her an asylum in her family; but she would not leave me. 'We are all the world to each other,' said she. 'I thank God, I have health and spirits to improve the talents with which nature has endowed me; and I trust if I employ them in the support of a beloved parent, I shall not be thought an unprofitable servant. While he lives, I pray for strength to pursue my employment; and when it pleases heaven to take one of us, may it give the survivor resignation to bear the separation as we ought: till then I will never leave him.'"

"But where is this inhuman persecutor?" said Temple.

"He has been abroad ever since," replied the old man; "but he has left orders with his lawyer never to give up the note till the utmost farthing is paid."

"And how much is the amount of your debts in all?" said Temple.

"Five hundred pounds," he replied.

Temple started: it was more than he expected. "But something must be done," said he: "that sweet maid must not wear out her life in a prison. I will see you again to-morrow, my friend," said he, shaking Eldridge's hand: "keep up your spirits: light and shade are not more happily blended than are the pleasures and pains of life; and the horrors of the one serve only to increase the splendor of the other."

"You never lost a wife and son," said Eldridge.

"No," replied he, "but I can feel for those that have." Eldridge pressed his hand as they went toward the door, and they parted in silence.

When they got without the walls of the prison, Temple thanked his friend Blakeney for introducing him to so worthy a character; and telling him he had a particular engagement in the city, wished him a good evening.

"And what is to be done for this distressed man," said Temple, as he walked up Ludgate Hill. "Would to heaven I had a fortune that would enable me instantly to discharge his debt: what exquisite transport, to see the expressive eyes of Lucy beaming at once with pleasure for her father's deliverance, and gratitude for her deliverer: but is not my fortune affluence," continued he, "nay superfluous wealth, when compared to the extreme indigence of Eldridge; and what have I done to deserve ease and plenty, while a brave worthy officer starves in a prison? Three hundred a year is surely sufficient for all my wants and wishes: at any rate Eldridge must be relieved."

When the heart has will, the hands can soon find means to execute a good action.

Temple was a young man, his feelings warm and impetuous; unacquainted with the world, his heart had not been rendered callous by being convinced of its fraud and hypocrisy. He pitied their sufferings, overlooked their faults, thought every bosom as generous as his own, and would chearfully have divided his last guinea with an unfortunate fellow creature.

No wonder, then, that such a man (without waiting a moment for the interference of Madam Prudence) should resolve to raise money sufficient for the relief of Eldridge, by mortgaging part of his fortune.

We will not enquire too minutely into the cause which might actuate him in this instance: suffice it to say, he immediately put the plan in execution; and in three days from the time he first saw the unfortunate Lieutenant, he had the superlative felicity of seeing him at liberty, and receiving an ample reward in the tearful eye and half articulated thanks of the grateful Lucy.

"And pray, young man," said his father to him one morning, "what are your designs in visiting thus constantly that old man and his daughter?"

Temple was at a loss for a reply: he had never asked himself the question: he hesitated; and his father continued –

"It was not till within these few days that I heard in what manner your acquaintance first commenced, and cannot suppose any thing but attachment to the daughter could carry you such imprudent lengths for the father: it certainly must be her art that drew you in to mortgage part of your fortune."

"Art, Sir!" cried Temple eagerly. "Lucy Eldridge is as free from art as she is from every other error: she is – "

"Everything that is amiable and lovely," said his father, interrupting him ironically: "no doubt in your opinion she is a pattern of excellence for all her sex to follow; but come, Sir, pray tell me what are your designs towards this paragon. I hope you do not intend to complete your folly by marrying her."

"Were my fortune such as would support her according to her merit, I don't know a woman more formed to insure happiness in the married state."

"Then prithee, my dear lad," said his father, "since your rank and fortune are so much beneath what your *Princess* might expect, be so kind as to turn your eyes on Miss Weatherby; who, having only an estate of three thousand a year, is more upon a level with you, and whose father yesterday solicited the mighty honour of your alliance. I shall leave you to consider on this offer; and pray remember, that your union with Miss Weatherby will put it in your power to be more liberally the friend of Lucy Eldridge."

The old gentleman walked in a stately manner out of the room; and Temple stood almost petrified with astonishment, contempt, and rage.

Chapter V.

Such Things Are

MISS WEATHERBY was the only child of a wealthy man, almost idolized by her parents, flattered by her dependants, and never contradicted even by those who called themselves her friends: I cannot give a better description than by the following lines.

> The lovely maid whose form and face
> Nature has deck'd with ev'ry grace,
> But in whose breast no virtues glow,
> Whose heart ne'er felt another's woe,
> Whose hand ne'er smooth'd the bed of pain,
> Or eas'd the captive's galling chain;
> But like the tulip caught the eye,
> Born just to be admir'd and die;
> When gone, no one regrets its loss,
> Or scarce remembers that it was.

Such was Miss Weatherby: her form lovely as nature could make it, but her mind uncultivated, her heart unfeeling, her passions impetuous, and her brain almost turned with flattery, dissipation, and pleasure; and such was the girl, whom a partial grandfather left independent mistress of the fortune before mentioned.

She had seen Temple frequently; and fancying she could never be happy without him, nor once imagining he could refuse a girl of her beauty and fortune, she prevailed on her fond father to offer the alliance to the old Earl of D —, Mr. Temple's father.

The Earl had received the offer courteously: he thought it a great match for Henry; and was too fashionable a man to suppose a wife could be any impediment to the friendship he professed for Eldridge and his daughter.

Unfortunately for Temple, he thought quite otherwise: the conversation he had just had with his father, discovered to him the situation of his heart; and he found that the most affluent fortune would bring no increase of happiness unless Lucy Eldridge shared it with him; and the knowledge of the purity of her sentiments, and the integrity of his own heart, made him shudder at the idea his father had started, of marrying a woman for no other reason than because the affluence of her fortune would enable him to injure her by maintaining in splendor the woman to whom his heart was devoted: he therefore resolved to refuse Miss Weatherby, and be the event what it might, offer his heart and hand to Lucy Eldridge.

Full of this determination, he sought his father, declared his resolution, and was commanded never more to appear in his presence. Temple bowed; his heart was too full to permit him to speak; he left the house precipitately, and hastened to relate the cause of his sorrows to his good old friend and his amiable daughter.

In the mean time, the Earl, vexed to the soul that such a fortune should be lost, determined to offer himself a candidate for Miss Weatherby's favour.

What wonderful changes are wrought by that reigning power, ambition! the love-sick girl, when first she heard of Temple's refusal, wept, raved, tore her hair, and vowed to found a protestant nunnery with her fortune; and by commencing abbess, shut herself up from the sight of cruel ungrateful man for ever.

Her father was a man of the world: he suffered this first transport to subside, and then very deliberately unfolded to her the offers of the old Earl, expatiated on the many benefits arising from an elevated title, painted in glowing colours the surprise and vexation of Temple when he should see her figuring as a Countess and his mother-in-law, and begged her to consider well before she made any rash vows.

The *distressed* fair one dried her tears, listened patiently, and at length declared she believed the surest method to revenge the slight put on her by the son, would be to accept the father: so said so done, and in a few days she became the Countess D —.

Temple heard the news with emotion: he had lost his father's favour by avowing his passion for Lucy, and he saw now there was no hope of regaining it: "but he shall not make me miserable," said he. "Lucy and I have no ambitious notions: we can live on three hundred a year for some little time, till the mortgage is paid off, and then we shall have sufficient not only for the comforts but many of the little elegancies of life. We will purchase a little cottage, my Lucy," said he, "and thither with your reverend father we will retire; we will forget there are such things as splendor, profusion, and dissipation: we will have some cows, and you shall be queen of the dairy; in a morning, while I look after my garden, you shall take a basket on your arm, and sally forth to feed your poultry; and as they flutter round you in token of humble gratitude, your father shall smoke his pipe in a woodbine alcove, and viewing the serenity of your countenance, feel such real pleasure dilate his own heart, as shall make him forget he had ever been unhappy."

Lucy smiled; and Temple saw it was a smile of approbation. He sought and found a cottage suited to his taste; thither, attended by Love and Hymen,[2] the happy trio retired; where, during many years of uninterrupted felicity, they cast not a wish beyond the little boundaries of their own tenement. Plenty, and her handmaid, Prudence, presided at their board, Hospitality stood at their gate, Peace smiled on each face, Content reigned in each heart, and Love and Health strewed roses on their pillows.

Such were the parents of Charlotte Temple, who was the only pledge of their mutual love, and who, at the earnest entreaty of a particular friend, was permitted to finish the education her mother had begun, at Madame Du Pont's school, where we first introduced her to the acquaintance of the reader.

Chapter VI.

An Intriguing Teacher

MADAME DU PONT was a woman every way calculated to take the care of young ladies, had that care entirely devolved on herself; but it was impossible to attend the education of a numerous school without proper as-

2. *Hymen*: The god of marriage in Greek mythology.

sistants; and those assistants were not always the kind of people whose conversation and morals were exactly such as parents of delicacy and refinement would wish a daughter to copy. Among the teachers at Madame Du Pont's school, was Mademoiselle La Rue, who added to a pleasing person and insinuating address, a liberal education and the manners of a gentlewoman. She was recommended to the school by a lady whose humanity overstepped the bounds of discretion: for though she knew Miss La Rue had eloped from a convent with a young officer, and, on coming to England, had lived with several different men in open defiance of all moral and religious duties; yet, finding her reduced to the most abject want, and believing the penitence which she professed to be sincere, she took her into her own family, and from thence recommended her to Madame Du Pont, as thinking the situation more suitable for a woman of her abilities. But Mademoiselle possessed too much of the spirit of intrigue to remain long without adventures. At church, where she constantly appeared, her person attracted the attention of a young man who was upon a visit at a gentleman's seat in the neighbourhood: she had met him several times clandestinely; and being invited to come out that evening, and eat some fruit and pastry in a summer-house belonging to the gentleman he was visiting, and requested to bring some of the ladies with her, Charlotte being her favourite, was fixed on to accompany her.

The mind of youth eagerly catches at promised pleasure: pure and innocent by nature, it thinks not of the dangers lurking beneath those pleasures, till too late to avoid them: when Mademoiselle asked Charlotte to go with her, she mentioned the gentleman as a relation, and spoke in such high terms of the elegance of his gardens, the sprightliness of his conversation, and the liberality with which he ever entertained his guests, that Charlotte thought only of the pleasure she should enjoy in the visit, – not on the imprudence of going without her governess's knowledge, or of the danger to which she exposed herself in visiting the house of a gay young man of fashion.

Madame Du Pont was gone out for the evening, and the rest of the ladies retired to rest, when Charlotte and the teacher stole out at the back gate, and in crossing the field, were accosted by Montraville, as mentioned in the first chapter.

Charlotte was disappointed in the pleasure she had promised herself from this visit. The levity of the gentlemen and the freedom of their conversation disgusted her. She was astonished at the liberties Mademoiselle permitted them to take; grew thoughtful and uneasy, and heartily wished herself at home again in her own chamber.

Perhaps one cause of that wish might be, an earnest desire to see the contents of the letter which had been put into her hand by Montraville.

Any reader who has the least knowledge of the world, will easily imagine the letter was made up of encomiums on her beauty, and vows of everlasting love and constancy; nor will he be surprised that a heart open to every gentle, generous sentiment, should feel itself warmed by gratitude for a man who professed to feel so much for her; nor is it improbable but her mind might revert to the agreeable person and martial appearance of Montraville.

In affairs of love, a young heart is never in more danger than when attempted by a handsome young soldier. A man of an indifferent appearance, will, when arrayed in a military habit, shew to advantage; but when beauty of person, elegance of manner, and an easy method of paying compliments, are united to the scarlet coat, smart cockade, and military sash, ah! well-a-day for the poor girl who gazes on him: she is in imminent danger; but if she listens to him with pleasure, 'tis all over with her, and from that moment she has neither eyes nor ears for any other object.

Now, my dear sober matron, (if a sober matron should deign to turn over these pages, before she trusts them to the eye of a darling daughter,) let me intreat you not to put on a grave face, and throw down the book in a passion and declare 'tis enough to turn the heads of half the girls in England; I do solemnly protest, my dear madam, I mean no more by what I have here advanced, than to ridicule those romantic girls, who foolishly imagine a red coat and silver epaulet constitute the fine gentleman; and should that fine gentleman make half a dozen fine speeches to them, they will imagine themselves so much in love as to fancy it a meritorious action to jump out of a two pair of stairs window, abandon their friends, and trust entirely to the honour of a man, who perhaps hardly knows the meaning of the word, and if he does, will be too much the modern man of refinement, to practice it in their favour.

Gracious heaven! when I think on the miseries that must rend the heart of a doating parent, when he sees the darling of his age at first seduced from his protection, and afterwards abandoned, by the very wretch whose promises of love decoyed her from the paternal roof – when he sees her poor and wretched, her bosom torn between remorse for her crime and love for her vile betrayer – when fancy paints to me the good old man stooping to raise the weeping penitent, while every tear from her eye is numbered by drops from his bleeding heart, my bosom glows with honest indignation, and I wish for power to extirpate those monsters of seduction from the earth.

Oh my dear girls—for to such only am I writing—listen not to the voice of love, unless sanctioned by paternal approbation: be assured, it is now past the days of romance: no woman can be run away with contrary to her own inclination: then kneel down each morning, and request kind heaven to keep you free from temptation, or, should it please to suffer you to be tried, pray for fortitude to resist the impulse of inclination when it runs counter to the precepts of religion and virtue.

Chapter VII.

Natural Sense of Propriety Inherent in the Female Bosom

"I CANNOT THINK we have done exactly right in going out this evening, Mademoiselle," said Charlotte, seating herself when she entered her apartment: "nay, I am sure it was not right; for I expected to be very happy, but was sadly disappointed."

"It was your own fault, then," replied Mademoiselle: "for I am sure my cousin omitted nothing that could serve to render the evening agreeable."

"True," said Charlotte: "but I thought the gentlemen were very free in their manner: I wonder you would suffer them to behave as they did."

"Prithee, don't be such a foolish little prude," said the artful woman, affecting anger: "I invited you to go in hopes it would divert you, and be an agreeable change of scene; however, if your delicacy was hurt by the behaviour of the gentlemen, you need not go again; so there let it rest."

"I do not intend to go again," said Charlotte, gravely taking off her bonnet, and beginning to prepare for bed: "I am sure, if Madame Du Pont knew we had been out to-night, she would be very angry; and it is ten to one but she hears of it by some means or other."

"Nay, Miss," said La Rue, "perhaps your mighty sense of propriety may lead you to tell her yourself: and in order to avoid the censure you would incur, should she hear of it by accident, throw the blame on me: but I confess I deserve it: it will be a very kind return for that partiality which led me to prefer you before any of the rest of the ladies; but perhaps it will give you pleasure," continued she, letting fall some hypocritical tears, "to see me deprived of bread, and for an action which by the most rigid could only be esteemed an inadvertency, lose my place and character, and be driven again into the world, where I have already suffered all the evils attendant on poverty."

This was touching Charlotte in the most vulnerable part: she rose from her seat, and taking Mademoiselle's hand—"You know, my dear La Rue," said she, "I love you too well, to do anything that would injure you in my governess's opinion: I am only sorry we went out this evening."

"I don't believe it, Charlotte," said she, assuming a little vivacity; "for if you had not gone out, you would not have seen the gentleman who met us crossing the field; and I rather think you were pleased with his conversation."

"I had seen him once before," replied Charlotte, "and thought him an agreeable man; and you know one is always pleased to see a person with whom one has passed several chearful hours. But," said she pausing, and drawing the letter from her pocket, while a gentle suffusion of vermillion tinged her neck and face, "he gave me this letter; what shall I do with it?"

"Read it, to be sure," returned Mademoiselle.

"I am afraid I ought not," said Charlotte: "my mother has often told me, I should never read a letter given me by a young man, without first giving it to her."

"Lord bless you, my dear girl," cried the teacher smiling, "have you a mind to be in leading strings all your life time. Prithee open the letter, read it, and judge for yourself; if you show it [to] your mother, the consequence will be, you will be taken from school, and a strict guard kept over you; so you will stand no chance of ever seeing the smart young officer again."

"I should not like to leave school yet," replied Charlotte, "till I have attained a greater proficiency in my Italian and music. But you can, if you please, Mademoiselle, take the letter back to Montraville, and tell him I wish him well, but cannot, with any propriety, enter into a clandestine correspondence with him." She laid the letter on the table, and began to undress herself.

"Well," said La Rue, "I vow you are an unaccountable girl: have you no curiosity to see the inside now? for my part I could no more let a letter addressed to me lie unopened so long, than I could work miracles: he writes a good hand," continued she, turning the letter, to look at the superscription.

"'Tis well enough," said Charlotte, drawing it towards her.

"He is a genteel young fellow," said La Rue carelessly, folding up her apron at the same time; "but I think he is marked with the smallpox."

"Oh you are greatly mistaken," said Charlotte eagerly; "he has a remarkable clear skin and fine complexion."

"His eyes, if I could judge by what I saw," said La Rue, "are grey and want expression."

"By no means," replied Charlotte; "they are the most expressive eyes I ever saw."

"Well, child, whether they are grey or black is of no consequence: you have determined not to read his letter; so it is likely you will never either see or hear from him again."

Charlotte took up the letter, and Mademoiselle continued –

"He is most probably going to America; and if ever you should hear any account of him, it may possibly be that he is killed; and though he loved you ever so fervently, though his last breath should be spent in a prayer for your happiness, it can be nothing to you: you can feel nothing for the fate of the man, whose letters you will not open, and whose sufferings you will not alleviate, by permitting him to think you would remember him when absent, and pray for his safety."

Charlotte still held the letter in her hand: her heart swelled at the conclusion of Mademoiselle's speech, and a tear dropped upon the wafer that closed it.[3]

"The wafer is not dry yet," said she, "and sure there can be no great harm –" She hesitated. La Rue was silent. "I may read it, Mademoiselle, and return it afterwards."

"Certainly," replied Mademoiselle.

"At any rate I am determined not to answer it," continued Charlotte, as she opened the letter.

Here let me stop to make one remark, and trust me my very heart aches while I write it; but certain I am, that when once a woman has stifled the sense of shame in her own bosom, when once she has lost sight of the basis on which reputation, honour, every thing that should be dear to the female heart, rests, she grows hardened in guilt, and will spare no pains to bring down innocence and beauty to the shocking level with herself: and this proceeds from that diabolical spirit of envy, which repines at seeing another in the full possession of that respect and esteem which she can no longer hope to enjoy.

Mademoiselle eyed the unsuspecting Charlotte, as she perused the letter, with a malignant pleasure. She saw, that the contents had awakened

---

3. *wafer*: A small disk of adhesive material used to seal papers.

new emotions in her youthful bosom: she encouraged her hopes, calmed her fears, and before they parted for the night, it was determined that she should meet Montraville the ensuing evening.

Chapter VIII.

Domestic Pleasures Planned

"I THINK, MY DEAR," said Mrs. Temple, laying her hand on her husband's arm as they were walking together in the garden, "I think next Wednesday is Charlotte's birth day: now I have formed a little scheme in my own mind, to give her an agreeable surprise; and if you have no objection, we will send for her home on that day." Temple pressed his wife's hand in token of approbation, and she proceeded. – "You know the little alcove at the bottom of the garden, of which Charlotte is so fond? I have an inclination to deck this out in a fanciful manner and invite all her little friends to partake of a collation of fruit, sweetmeats, and other things suitable to the general taste of young guests; and to make it more pleasing to Charlotte, she shall be mistress of the feast, and entertain her visitors in this alcove. I know she will be delighted; and to complete all, they shall have some music, and finish with a dance."

"A very fine plan, indeed," said Temple, smiling; "and you really suppose I will wink at your indulging the girl in this manner? You will quite spoil her, Lucy; indeed you will."

"She is the only child we have," said Mrs. Temple, the whole tenderness of a mother adding animation to her fine countenance; but it was withal tempered so sweetly with the meek affection and submissive duty of the wife, that as she paused expecting her husband's answer, he gazed at her tenderly, and found he was unable to refuse her request.

"She is a good girl," said Temple.

"She is, indeed," replied the fond mother exultingly, "a grateful, affectionate girl; and I am sure will never lose sight of the duty she owes her parents."

"If she does," said he, "she must forget the example set her by the best of mothers."

Mrs. Temple could not reply; but the delightful sensation that dilated her heart sparkled in her intelligent eyes and heightened the vermillion on her cheeks.

Of all the pleasures of which the human mind is sensible, there is none equal to that which warms and expands the bosom, when listening to commendations bestowed on us by a beloved object, and are conscious of having deserved them.

Ye giddy flutterers in the fantastic round of dissipation, who eagerly seek pleasure in the lofty dome, rich treat, and midnight revel – tell me, ye thoughtless daughters of folly, have ye ever found the phantom you have so long sought with such unremitted assiduity? Has she not always eluded your grasp, and when you have reached your hand to take the cup she extends to her deluded votaries, have you not found the long-expected draught strongly tinctured with the bitter dregs of disappointment? I know you have: I see it in the wan cheek, sunk eye, and air of chagrin, which ever mark the children of dissipation. Pleasure is a vain illusion; she draws you on to a thousand follies, errors, and I may say vices, and then leaves you to deplore your thoughtless credulity.

Look, my dear friends, at yonder lovely Virgin, arrayed in a white robe devoid of ornament; behold the meekness of her countenance, the modesty of her gait; her handmaids are *Humility, Filial Piety, Conjugal Affection, Industry,* and *Benevolence*; her name is *Content*; she holds in her hand the cup of true felicity, and when once you have formed an intimate acquaintance with these her attendants, nay you must admit them as your bosom friends and chief counsellors, then, whatever may be your situation in life, the meek eyed Virgin will immediately take up her abode with you.

Is poverty your portion? – she will lighten your labours, preside at your frugal board, and watch your quiet slumbers.

Is your state mediocrity? – she will heighten every blessing you enjoy, by informing you how grateful you should be to that bountiful Providence who might have placed you in the most abject situation; and, by teaching you to weigh your blessings against your deserts, show you how much more you receive than you have a right to expect.

Are you possessed of affluence? – what an inexhaustible fund of happiness will she lay before you! To relieve the distressed, redress the injured, in short, to perform all the good works of peace and mercy.

Content, my dear friends, will blunt even the arrows of adversity, so that they cannot materially harm you. She will dwell in the humblest cottage; she will attend you even to a prison. Her parent is Religion; her sisters, Patience and Hope. She will pass with you through life, smoothing the rough paths and tread to earth those thorns which every one must meet with as they journey onward to the appointed goal. She will soften the pains of sickness, continue with you even in the cold gloomy hour of death, and, chearing you with the smiles of her heaven-born sister, Hope, lead you triumphant to a blissfull eternity.

I confess I have rambled strangely from my story: but what of that? if I have been so lucky as to find the road to happiness, why should I be such a niggard as to omit so good an opportunity of pointing out the way to others. The very basis of true peace of mind is a benevolent wish to see all the world as happy as one's self; and from my soul do I pity the selfish churl, who, remembering the little bickerings of anger, envy, and fifty other disagreeables to which frail mortality is subject, would wish to revenge the affront which pride whispers him he has received. For my own part, I can safely declare, there is not a human being in the universe, whose prosperity I should not rejoice in, and to whose happiness I would not contribute to the utmost limit of my power: and may my offences be no more remembered in the day of general retribution, than as from my soul I forgive every offence or injury received from a fellow creature.

Merciful heaven! who would exchange the rapture of such a reflexion for all the gaudy tinsel which the world calls pleasure!

But to return. – Content dwelt in Mrs. Temple's bosom, and spread a charming animation over her countenance, as her husband led her in, to lay the plan she had formed (for the celebration of Charlotte's birth day,) before Mr. Eldridge.

Chapter IX.

We Know Not What a Day May Bring Forth

VARIOUS WERE the sensations which agitated the mind of Charlotte, during the day preceding the evening in which she was to meet Montraville. Several times did she almost resolve to go to her governess, show her the letter, and be guided by her advice: but Charlotte had taken one step in the ways of imprudence; and when that is once done, there are always innumerable obstacles to prevent the erring person returning to the path of rectitude: yet these obstacles, however forcible they may appear in general, exist chiefly in imagination.

Charlotte feared the anger of her governess: she loved her mother, and the very idea of incurring her displeasure, gave her the greatest uneasiness: but there was a more forcible reason still remaining: should she show the letter to Madame Du Pont, she must confess the means by which it came into her possession; and what would be the consequence? Mademoiselle would be turned out of doors.

"I must not be ungrateful," said she. "La Rue is very kind to me; besides I can, when I see Montraville, inform him of the impropriety of our continuing to see or correspond with each other, and request him to come no more to Chichester."

However prudent Charlotte might be in these resolutions, she certainly did not take a proper method to confirm herself in them. Several times in the course of the day, she indulged herself in reading over the letter, and each time she read it, the contents sunk deeper in her heart. As evening drew near, she caught herself frequently consulting her watch. "I wish this foolish meeting was over," said she, by way of apology to her own heart, "I wish it was over; for when I have seen him, and convinced him my resolution is not to be shaken, I shall feel my mind much easier."

The appointed hour arrived. Charlotte and Mademoiselle eluded the eye of vigilance; and Montraville, who had waited their coming with impatience, received them with rapturous and unbounded acknowledgments for their condescension: he had wisely brought Belcour with him to entertain Mademoiselle, while he enjoyed an uninterrupted conversation with Charlotte.

Belcour was a man whose character might be comprised in a few words; and as he will make some figure in the ensuing pages, I shall here describe him. He possessed a genteel fortune, and had a liberal education; dissipated, thoughtless, and capricious, he paid little regard to the moral duties, and less to religious ones: eager in the pursuit of pleasure, he minded not the miseries he inflicted on others, provided his own wishes, however extravagant, were gratified. Self, darling self, was the idol he worshipped, and to that he would have sacrificed the interest and happiness of all mankind. Such was the friend of Montraville: will not the reader be ready to imagine, that the man who could regard such a character, must be actuated by the same feelings, follow the same pursuits, and be equally unworthy with the person to whom he thus gave his confidence?

But Montraville was a different character: generous in his disposition, liberal in his opinions, and good-natured almost to a fault; yet eager and impetuous in the pursuit of a favorite object, he staid not to reflect on the consequence which might follow the attainment of his wishes; with a mind ever open to conviction, had he been so fortunate as to possess a friend who would have pointed out the cruelty of endeavouring to gain the heart of an innocent artless girl, when he knew it was utterly impossible for him to marry her, and when the gratification of his passion would be unavoidable infamy and misery to her, and a cause of never-ceasing remorse to himself: had these dreadful consequences been placed before him in a proper light, the humanity of his nature would have urged him to give up the pursuit: but Belcour was not this friend; he rather encouraged the growing passion of Montraville; and being pleased with the vivacity of Mademoiselle, resolved to leave no argument untried, which he thought might prevail on her to be the companion of their intended voyage; and he made no doubt but her example, added to the rhetoric of Montraville, would persuade Charlotte to go with them.

Charlotte had, when she went out to meet Montraville, flattered herself that her resolution was not to be shaken, and that, conscious of the impropriety of her conduct in having a clandestine intercourse with a stranger, she would never repeat the indiscretion.

But alas! poor Charlotte, she knew not the deceitfulness of her own heart, or she would have avoided the trial of her stability.

Montraville was tender, eloquent, ardent, and yet respectful. "Shall I not see you once more," said he, "before I leave England? will you not bless me by an assurance, that when we are divided by a vast expanse of sea I shall not be forgotten?"

Charlotte sighed.

"Why that sigh, my dear Charlotte? could I flatter myself that a fear for my safety, or a wish for my welfare occasioned it, how happy would it make me."

"I shall ever wish you well, Montraville," said she; "but we must meet no more."

"Oh say not so, my lovely girl: reflect, that when I leave my native land, perhaps a few short weeks may terminate my existence; the perils of the ocean – the dangers of war – "

"I can hear no more," said Charlotte in a tremulous voice. "I must leave you."

"Say you will see me once again."

"I dare not," said she.

"Only for one half hour to-morrow evening: 'tis my last request. I shall never trouble you again, Charlotte."

"I know not what to say," cried Charlotte, struggling to draw her hands from him: "let me leave you now."

"And you will come to-morrow," said Montraville.

"Perhaps I may," said she.

"Adieu then. I will live upon that hope till we meet again."

CHAPTER X. WHEN WE HAVE EXCITED CURIOSITY 63

He kissed her hand. She sighed an adieu, and catching hold of Mademoiselle's arm, hastily entered the garden gate.

Chapter X.

When We Have Excited Curiosity, It Is but an Act of Good Nature to Gratify It

MONTRAVILLE WAS the youngest son of a gentleman of fortune, whose family being numerous, he was obliged to bring up his sons to genteel professions, by the exercise of which they might hope to raise themselves into notice.

"My daughters," said he, "have been educated like gentlewomen; and should I die before they are settled, they must have some provision made, to place them above the snares and temptations which vice ever holds out to the elegant, accomplished female, when oppressed by the frowns of poverty and the sting of dependance: my boys, with only moderate incomes, when placed in the church, at the bar, or in the field, may exert their talents, make themselves friends, and raise their fortunes on the basis of merit."

When Montraville chose the profession of arms, his father presented him with a commission, and made him a handsome provision for his private purse. "Now, my boy," said he, "go! seek glory in the field of battle. You have received from me all I shall ever have it in my power to bestow: it is certain I have interest to gain you promotion; but be assured that interest shall never be exerted, unless by your future conduct you deserve it. Remember, therefore, your success in life depends entirely on yourself. There is one thing I think it my duty to caution you against; the precipitancy with which young men frequently rush into matrimonial engagements, and by their thoughtlessness draw many a deserving woman into scenes of poverty and distress. A soldier has no business to think of a wife till his rank is such as to place him above the fear of bringing into the world a train of helpless innocents, heirs only to penury and affliction. If, indeed, a woman, whose fortune is sufficient to preserve you in that state of independence I would teach you to prize, should generously bestow herself on a young soldier, whose chief hope of future prosperity depended on his success in the field – if such a woman should offer – every barrier is removed, and I should rejoice in an union which would promise so much felicity. But mark me, boy, if, on the contrary, you rush into a precipitate union with a girl of little or no fortune, take the poor creature from a comfortable home and kind friends and plunge her into all the evils a narrow income and increasing family can inflict, I will leave you to enjoy the blessed fruits of your rashness; for by all that is sacred, neither my interest or fortune shall ever be exerted in your favour. I am serious," continued he, "therefore imprint this conversation on your memory, and let it influence your future conduct. Your happiness will always be dear to me; and I wish to warn you of a rock on which the peace of many an honest fellow has been wrecked; for believe me, the difficulties and dangers of the longest winter campaign are much easier to be borne, than the pangs that would seize your heart, when you beheld the woman of your choice, the children of your affection, involved in penury and distress, and reflected that it was your own folly and precipitancy had been the prime cause of their sufferings."

As this conversation passed but a few hours before Montraville took leave of his father, it was deeply impressed on his mind: when, therefore, Belcour came with him to the place of assignation with Charlotte, he directed him to enquire of the French woman what were Miss Temple's expectations in regard to fortune.

Mademoiselle informed him, that though Charlotte's father possessed a genteel independence, it was by no means probable that he could give his daughter more than a thousand pounds; and in case she did not marry to his liking, it was possible he might not give her a single *sous*; nor did it appear the least likely, that Mr. Temple would agree to her union with a young man on the point of embarking for the seat of war.

Montraville therefore concluded it was impossible he should ever marry Charlotte Temple; and what end he proposed to himself by continuing the acquaintance he had commenced with her, he did not at that moment give himself time to enquire.

Chapter XI.

Conflict of Love and Duty

ALMOST A WEEK was now gone, and Charlotte continued every evening to meet Montraville, and in her heart every meeting was resolved to be the last; but alas! when Montraville at parting would earnestly intreat one more interview, that treacherous heart betrayed her; and, forgetful of its resolution, pleaded the cause of the enemy so powerfully, that Charlotte was unable to resist. Another and another meeting succeeded; and so well did Montraville improve each opportunity, that the heedless girl at length confessed no idea could be so painful to her as that of never seeing him again.

"Then we will never be parted," said he.

"Ah, Montraville," replied Charlotte, forcing a smile, "how can it be avoided? My parents would never consent to our union; and even could they be brought to approve it, how should I bear to be separated from my kind, my beloved mother?"

"Then you love your parents more than you do me, Charlotte?"

"I hope I do," said she, blushing and looking down, "I hope my affection for them will ever keep me from infringing the laws of filial duty."

"Well, Charlotte," said Montraville gravely, and letting go her hand, "since that is the case, I find I have deceived myself with fallacious hopes. I had flattered my fond heart, that I was dearer to Charlotte than any thing in the world beside. I thought that you would for my sake have braved the dangers of the ocean, that you would, by your affection and smiles, have softened the hardships of war, and, had it been my fate to fall, that your tenderness would chear the hour of death, and smooth my passage to another world. But farewel, Charlotte! I see you never loved me. I shall now welcome the friendly ball that deprives me of the sense of my misery."

"Oh stay, unkind Montraville," cried she, catching hold of his arm, as he pretended to leave her, "stay, and to calm your fears, I will here protest that was it not for the fear of giving pain to the best of parents, and returning their kindness with ingratitude, I would follow you through every danger, and, in studying to promote your happiness, insure my own. But I cannot break my mother's heart, Montraville; I must not bring the grey hairs of my doating grand-father with sorrow to the grave, or make my beloved father perhaps curse the hour that gave me birth." She covered her face with her hands, and burst into tears.

"All these distressing scenes, my dear Charlotte," cried Montraville, "are merely the chimeras of a disturbed fancy. Your parents might perhaps grieve at first; but when they heard from your own hand that you was with a man of honour, and that it was to insure your felicity by an union with him, to which you feared they would never have given their assent, that you left their protection, they will, be assured, forgive an error which love alone occasioned, and when we return from America, receive you with open arms and tears of joy."

Belcour and Mademoiselle heard this last speech, and conceiving it a proper time to throw in their advice and persuasions, approached Charlotte, and so well seconded the entreaties of Montraville, that finding Mademoiselle intended going with Belcour, and feeling her own treacherous heart too much inclined to accompany them, the hapless Charlotte, in an evil hour, consented that the next evening they should bring a chaise to the end of the town, and that she would leave her friends, and throw herself entirely on the protection of Montraville. "But should you," said she, looking earnestly at him, her eyes full of tears, "should you, forgetful of your promises, and repenting the engagements you here voluntarily enter into, forsake and leave me on a foreign shore – "

"Judge not so meanly of me," said he. "The moment we reach our place of destination, Hymen shall sanctify our love; and when I shall forget your goodness, may heaven forget me."

"Ah," said Charlotte, leaning on Mademoiselle's arm as they walked up the garden together, "I have forgot all that I ought to have remembered, in consenting to this intended elopement."

"You are a strange girl," said Mademoiselle: "you never know your ownmind two minutes at a time. Just now you declared Montraville's happiness was what you prized most in the world; and now I suppose you repent having insured that happiness by agreeing to accompany him abroad."

"Indeed I do repent," replied Charlotte, "from my soul: but while discretion points out the impropriety of my conduct, inclination urges me on to ruin."

"Ruin! fiddlestick!" said Mademoiselle; "am I not going with you? and do I feel any of these qualms?"

"You do not renounce a tender father and mother," said Charlotte.

"But I hazard my dear reputation," replied Mademoiselle, bridling.

"True," replied Charlotte, "but you do not feel what I do." She then bade her good night: but sleep was a stranger to her eyes, and the tear of anguish watered her pillow.

Chapter XII.

Nature's last, best gift:
Creature in whom excell'd, whatever could
To sight or thought be nam'd!

Holy, divine! good, amiable, and sweet!
How thou art fall'n! —

WHEN CHARLOTTE left her restless bed, her languid eye and pale cheek discovered to Madame Du Pont the little repose she had tasted.

"My dear child," said the affectionate governess, "what is the cause of the languor so apparent in your frame? Are you not well?"

"Yes, my dear Madam, very well," replied Charlotte, attempting to smile, "but I know not how it was; I could not sleep last night, and my spirits are depressed this morning."

"Come chear up, my love," said the governess; "I believe I have brought a cordial to revive them. I have just received a letter from your good mama, and here is one for yourself."

Charlotte hastily took the letter: it contained these words —

"As to-morrow is the anniversary of the happy day that gave my beloved girl to the anxious wishes of a maternal heart, I have requested your governess to let you come home and spend it with us; and as I know you to be a good affectionate child, and make it your study to improve in those branches of education which you know will give most pleasure to your delighted parents, as a reward for your diligence and attention I have prepared an agreeable surprise for your reception. Your grand-father, eager to embrace the darling of his aged heart, will come in the chaise for you; so hold yourself in readiness to attend him by nine o'clock. Your dear father joins in every tender wish for your health and future felicity, which warms the heart of my dear Charlotte's affectionate mother,

L. TEMPLE."

"Gracious heaven!" cried Charlotte, forgetting where she was, and raising her streaming eyes as in earnest supplication.

Madame Du Pont was surprised. "Why these tears, my love?" said she. "Why this seeming agitation? I thought the letter would have rejoiced, instead of distressing you."

"It does rejoice me," replied Charlotte, endeavouring at composure, "but I was praying for merit to deserve the unremitted attentions of the best of parents."

"You do right," said Madame Du Pont, "to ask the assistance of heaven that you may continue to deserve their love. Continue, my dear

Charlotte, in the course you have ever pursued, and you will insure at once their happiness and your own."

"Oh!" cried Charlotte, as her governess left her, "I have forfeited both for ever! Yet let me reflect:—the irrevocable step is not yet taken: it is not too late to recede from the brink of a precipice, from which I can only behold the dark abyss of ruin, shame, and remorse!"

She arose from her seat, and flew to the apartment of La Rue. "Oh Mademoiselle!" said she, "I am snatched by a miracle from destruction! This letter has saved me: it has opened my eyes to the folly I was so near committing. I will not go, Mademoiselle; I will not wound the hearts of those dear parents who make my happiness the whole study of their lives."

"Well," said Mademoiselle, "do as you please, Miss; but pray understand that my resolution is taken, and it is not in your power to alter it. I shall meet the gentlemen at the appointed hour, and shall not be surprized at any outrage which Montraville may commit, when he finds himself disappointed. Indeed I should not be astonished, was he to come immediately here, and reproach you for your instability in the hearing of the whole school: and what will be the consequence? you will bear the odium of having formed the resolution of eloping, and every girl of spirit will laugh at your want of fortitude to put it in execution, while prudes and fools will load you with reproach and contempt. You will have lost the confidence of your parents, incurred their anger, and the scoffs of the world; and what fruit do you expect to reap from this piece of heroism, (for such no doubt you think it is?) you will have the pleasure to reflect, that you have deceived the man who adores you, and whom in your heart you prefer to all other men, and that you are separated from him for ever."

This eloquent harangue was given with such volubility, that Charlotte could not find an opportunity to interrupt her, or to offer a single word till the whole was finished, and then found her ideas so confused, that she knew not what to say.

At length she determined that she would go with Mademoiselle to the place of assignation, convince Montraville of the necessity of adhering to the resolution of remaining behind; assure him of her affection, and bid him adieu.

Charlotte formed this plan in her mind, and exulted in the certainty of its success. "How shall I rejoice," said she, "in this triumph of reason over inclination, and, when in the arms of my affectionate parents, lift up my soul in gratitude to heaven as I look back on the dangers I have escaped!"

The hour of assignation arrived: Mademoiselle put what money and valuables she possessed in her pocket, and advised Charlotte to do the same; but she refused; "my resolution is fixed," said she; "I will sacrifice love to duty."

Mademoiselle smiled internally; and they proceeded softly down the back stairs and out of the garden gate. Montraville and Belcour were ready to receive them.

"Now," said Montraville, taking Charlotte in his arms, "you are mine for ever."

"No," said she, withdrawing from his embrace, "I am come to take an everlasting farewel."

It would be useless to repeat the conversation that here ensued; suffice it to say, that Montraville used every argument that had formerly been successful, Charlotte's resolution began to waver, and he drew her almost imperceptibly towards the chaise.

"I cannot go," said she: "cease, dear Montraville, to persuade. I must not: religion, duty, forbid."

"Cruel Charlotte," said he, "if you disappoint my ardent hopes, by all that is sacred, this hand shall put a period to my existence. I cannot – will not live without you."

"Alas! my torn heart!" said Charlotte, "how shall I act?"

"Let me direct you," said Montraville, lifting her into the chaise.

"Oh! my dear forsaken parents!" cried Charlotte.

The chaise drove off. She shrieked, and fainted into the arms of her betrayer.

Chapter XIII.

Cruel Disappointment

"WHAT PLEASURE," cried Mr. Eldridge, as he stepped into the chaise to go for his grand-daughter, "what pleasure expands the heart of an old man when he beholds the progeny of a beloved child growing up in every virtue that adorned the minds of her parents. I foolishly thought, some few years since, that every sense of joy was buried in the graves of my dear partner and my son; but my Lucy, by her filial affection, soothed my soul to peace, and this dear Charlotte has twined herself round my heart, and opened such new scenes of delight to my view, that I almost forget I have ever been unhappy."

When the chaise stopped, he alighted with the alacrity of youth; so much do the emotions of the soul influence the body.

It was half past eight o'clock; the ladies were assembled in the school room, and Madame Du Pont was preparing to offer the morning sacrifice of prayer and praise, when it was discovered, that Mademoiselle and Charlotte were missing.

"She is busy, no doubt," said the governess, "in preparing Charlotte for her little excursion; but pleasure should never make us forget our duty to our Creator. Go, one of you, and bid them both attend prayers."

The lady who went to summon them, soon returned, and informed the governess, that the room was locked, and that she had knocked repeatedly, but obtained no answer.

"Good heaven!" cried Madame Du Pont, "this is very strange:" and turning pale with terror, she went hastily to the door, and ordered it to be forced open. The apartment instantly discovered, that no person had been in it the preceding night, the beds appearing as though just made. The house was instantly a scene of confusion: the garden, the pleasure grounds were searched to no purpose, every apartment rang with the names of Miss Temple and Mademoiselle; but they were too distant to hear; and every face wore the marks of disappointment.

Mr. Eldridge was sitting in the parlour, eagerly expecting his grand-daughter to descend, ready equipped for her journey: he heard the confusion that reigned in the house; he heard the name of Charlotte frequently repeated. "What can be the matter?" said he, rising and opening the door: "I fear some accident has befallen my dear girl."

The governess entered. The visible agitation of her countenance discovered that something extraordinary had happened.

"Where is Charlotte?" said he, "Why does not my child come to welcome her doating parent?"

"Be composed, my dear Sir," said Madame Du Pont, "do not frighten yourself unnecessarily. She is not in the house at present; but as Mademoiselle is undoubtedly with her, she will speedily return in safety; and I hope they will both be able to account for this unseasonable absence in such a manner as shall remove our present uneasiness."

"Madam," cried the old man, with an angry look, "has my child been accustomed to go out without leave, with no other company or protector than that French woman. Pardon me, Madam, I mean no reflections on your country, but I never did like Mademoiselle La Rue; I think she was a very improper person to be entrusted with the care of such a girl as Charlotte Temple, or to be suffered to take her from under your immediate protection."

"You wrong me, Mr. Eldridge," replied she, "if you suppose I have ever permitted your grand-daughter to go out unless with the other ladies. I would to heaven I could form any probable conjecture concerning her absence this morning, but it is a mystery which her return can alone unravel."

Servants were now dispatched to every place where there was the least hope of hearing any tidings of the fugitives, but in vain. Dreadful were the hours of horrid suspense which Mr. Eldridge passed till twelve o'clock, when that suspense was reduced to a shocking certainty, and every spark of hope which till then they had indulged, was in a moment extinguished.

Mr. Eldridge was preparing, with a heavy heart, to return to his anxiously-expecting children, when Madame Du Pont received the following note without either name or date.

"Miss Temple is well, and wishes to relieve the anxiety of her parents, by letting them know she has voluntarily put herself under the protection of a man whose future study shall be to make her happy. Pursuit is needless; the measures taken to avoid discovery are too effectual to be eluded. When she thinks her friends are reconciled to this precipitate step, they may perhaps be informed of her place of residence. Mademoiselle is with her."

As Madame Du Pont read these cruel lines, she turned pale as ashes, her limbs trembled, and she was forced to call for a glass of water. She loved Charlotte truly; and when she reflected on the innocence and gentleness of her disposition, she concluded that it must have been the advice and machinations of La Rue, which led her to this imprudent action; she recollected her agitation at the receipt of her mother's letter, and saw in it the conflict of her mind.

"Does that letter relate to Charlotte?" said Mr. Eldridge, having waited some time in expectation of Madame Du Pont's speaking.

"It does," said she. "Charlotte is well, but cannot return today."

"Not return, Madam? where is she? who will detain her from her fond, expecting parents?"

"You distract me with these questions, Mr. Eldridge. Indeed I know not where she is, or who has seduced her from her duty."

The whole truth now rushed at once upon Mr. Eldridge's mind. "She has eloped then," said he. "My child is betrayed; the darling, the comfort of my aged heart, is lost. Oh would to heaven I had died but yesterday."

A violent gush of grief in some measure relieved him, and, after several vain attempts, he at length assumed sufficient composure to read the note.

"And how shall I return to my children?" said he: "how approach that mansion, so late the habitation of peace? Alas! my dear Lucy, how will you support these heart-rending tidings? or how shall I be enabled to console you, who need so much consolation myself?"

The old man returned to the chaise, but the light step and chearful countenance were no more; sorrow filled his heart, and guided his motions; he seated himself in the chaise, his venerable head reclined upon his bosom, his hands were folded, his eye fixed on vacancy, and the large drops of sorrow rolled silently down his cheeks. There was a mixture of anguish and resignation depicted in his countenance, as if he would say, henceforth who shall dare to boast his happiness, or even in idea contemplate his treasure, lest, in the very moment his heart is exulting in its own felicity, the object which constitutes that felicity should be torn from him.

Chapter XIV.

Maternal Sorrow

SLOW AND HEAVY passed the time while the carriage was conveying Mr. Eldridge home; and yet when he came in sight of the house, he wished a longer reprieve from the dreadful task of informing Mr. and Mrs. Temple of their daughter's elopement.

It is easy to judge the anxiety of these affectionate parents, when they found the return of their father delayed so much beyond the expected time. They were now met in the dining parlour, and several of the young people who had been invited were already arrived. Each different part of the company was employed in the same manner, looking out at the windows which faced the road. At length the long-expected chaise appeared. Mrs. Temple ran out to receive and welcome her darling: her young companions flocked round the door, each one eager to give her joy on the return of her birth-day. The door of the chaise was opened: Charlotte was not there. "Where is my child?" cried Mrs. Temple, in breathless agitation.

Mr. Eldridge could not answer: he took hold of his daughter's hand and led her into the house; and sinking on the first chair he came to, burst into tears, and sobbed aloud.

"She is dead," cried Mrs. Temple. "Oh my dear Charlotte!" and clasping her hands in an agony of distress, fell into strong hysterics.

Mr. Temple, who had stood speechless with surprize and fear, now ventured to enquire if indeed his Charlotte was no more. Mr. Eldridge led him into another apartment; and putting the fatal note into his hand, cried – "Bear it like a Christian," and turned from him, endeavouring to suppress his own too visible emotions.

It would be vain to attempt describing what Mr. Temple felt whilst he hastily ran over the dreadful lines: when he had finished, the paper dropt from his unnerved hand. "Gracious heaven!" said he, "could Charlotte act thus?" Neither tear nor sigh escaped him; and he sat the image of mute sorrow, till roused from his stupor by the repeated shrieks of Mrs. Temple. He rose hastily, and rushing into the apartment where she was, folded his arms about her, and saying – "Let us be patient, my dear Lucy," nature relieved his almost bursting heart by a friendly gush of tears.

Should any one, presuming on his own philosophic temper, look with an eye of contempt on the man who could indulge a woman's weakness, let him remember that man was a father, and he will then pity the misery which wrung those drops from a noble, generous heart.

Mrs. Temple beginning to be a little more composed, but still imagining her child was dead, her husband, gently taking her hand, cried – "You are mistaken, my love. Charlotte is not dead."

"Then she is very ill, else why did she not come? But I will go to her: the chaise is still at the door: let me go instantly to the dear girl. If I was ill, she would fly to attend me, to alleviate my sufferings, and chear me with her love."

"Be calm, my dearest Lucy, and I will tell you all," said Mr. Temple. "You must not go, indeed you must not; it will be of no use."

"Temple," said she, assuming a look of firmness and composure, "tell me the truth I beseech you. I cannot bear this dreadful suspense. What misfortune has befallen my child? Let me know the worst, and I will endeavour to bear it as I ought."

"Lucy," replied Mr. Temple, "imagine your daughter alive, and in no danger of death: what misfortune would you then dread?"

"There is one misfortune which is worse than death. But I know my child too well to suspect – "

"Be not too confident, Lucy."

"Oh heavens!" said she, "what horrid images do you start: is it possible she should forget – "

"She has forgot us all, my love; she has preferred the love of a stranger to the affectionate protection of her friends."

"Not eloped?" cried she eagerly.

Mr. Temple was silent.

"You cannot contradict it," said she. "I see my fate in those tearful eyes. Oh Charlotte! Charlotte! how ill have you requited our tenderness!

But, Father of Mercies," continued she, sinking on her knees, and raising her streaming eyes and clasped hands to heaven, "this once vouchsafe to hear a fond, a distracted mother's prayer. Oh let thy bounteous Providence watch over and protect the dear thoughtless girl, save her from the miseries which I fear will be her portion, and oh! of thine infinite mercy, make her not a mother, lest she should one day feel what I now suffer."

The last words faultered on her tongue, and she fell fainting into the arms of her husband, who had involuntarily dropped on his knees beside her.

A mother's anguish, when disappointed in her tenderest hopes, none but a mother can conceive. Yet, my dear young readers, I would have you read this scene with attention, and reflect that you may yourselves one day be mothers. Oh my friends, as you value your eternal happiness, wound not, by thoughtless ingratitude, the peace of the mother who bore you: remember the tenderness, the care, the unremitting anxiety with which she has attended to all your wants and wishes from earliest infancy to the present day; behold the mild ray of affectionate applause that beams from her eye on the performance of your duty: listen to her reproofs with silent attention; they proceed from a heart anxious for your future felicity: you must love her; nature, all-powerful nature, has planted the seeds of filial affection in your bosoms.

Then once more read over the sorrows of poor Mrs. Temple, and remember, the mother whom you so dearly love and venerate will feel the same, when you, forgetful of the respect due to your maker and yourself, forsake the paths of virtue for those of vice and folly.

Chapter XV.

Embarkation

IT WAS WITH THE UTMOST difficulty that the united efforts of Mademoiselle and Montraville could support Charlotte's spirits during their short ride from Chichester to Portsmouth, where a boat waited to take them immediately on board the ship in which they were to embark for America.

As soon as she became tolerably composed, she entreated pen and ink to write to her parents. This she did in the most affecting, artless manner, entreating their pardon and blessing, and describing the dreadful situation of her mind, the conflict she suffered in endeavouring to conquer this unfortunate attachment, and concluded with saying, her only hope of future comfort consisted in the (perhaps delusive) idea she indulged, of being once more folded in their protecting arms, and hearing the words of peace and pardon from their lips.

The tears streamed incessantly while she was writing, and she was frequently obliged to lay down her pen: but when the task was completed, and she had committed the letter to the care of Montraville to be sent to the post office, she became more calm, and indulging the delightful hope of soon receiving an answer that would seal her pardon, she in some measure assumed her usual chearfulness.

But Montraville knew too well the consequences that must unavoidably ensue, should this letter reach Mr. Temple: he therefore wisely resolved to walk on the deck, tear it in pieces, and commit the fragments to the care of Neptune, who might or might not, as it suited his convenience, convey them on shore.

All Charlotte's hopes and wishes were now concentred in one, namely that the fleet might be detained at Spithead till she could receive a letter from her friends: but in this she was disappointed, for the second morning after she went on board, the signal was made, the fleet weighed anchor, and in a few hours (the wind being favourable) they bid adieu to the white cliffs of Albion.[4]

In the mean time every enquiry that could be thought of was made by Mr. and Mrs. Temple; for many days did they indulge the fond hope that she was merely gone off to be married, and that when the indissoluble knot was once tied, she would return with the partner she had chosen, and entreat their blessing and forgiveness.

"And shall we not forgive her?" said Mr. Temple.

"Forgive her!" exclaimed the mother. "Oh yes, whatever be our errors, is she not our child? and though bowed to the earth even with shame and remorse, is it not our duty to raise the poor penitent, and whisper peace and comfort to her desponding soul? would she but return, with rapture would I fold her to my heart, and bury every remembrance of her faults in the dear embrace."

But still day after day passed on, and Charlotte did not appear, nor were any tidings to be heard of her: yet each rising morning was welcomed by some new hope – the evening brought with it disappointment. At length hope was no more; despair usurped her place; and the mansion which

---

4. *Albion*: An archaic name for Great Britain.

was once the mansion of peace, became the habitation of pale, dejected melancholy.

The chearful smile that was wont to adorn the face of Mrs. Temple was fled, and had it not been for the support of unaffected piety, and a consciousness of having ever set before her child the fairest example, she must have sunk under this heavy affliction.

"Since," said she, "the severest scrutiny cannot charge me with any breach of duty to have deserved this severe chastisement, I will bow before the power who inflicts it with humble resignation to his will; nor shall the duty of a wife be totally absorbed in the feelings of the mother; I will endeavour to appear more chearful, and by appearing in some measure to have conquered my own sorrow, alleviate the sufferings of my husband, and rouse him from that torpor into which this misfortune has plunged him. My father too demands my care and attention: I must not, by a selfish indulgence of my own grief, forget the interest those two dear objects take in my happiness or misery: I will wear a smile on my face, though the thorn rankles in my heart; and if by so doing, I in the smallest degree contribute to restore their peace of mind, I shall be amply rewarded for the pain the concealment of my own feelings may occasion."

Thus argued this excellent woman: and in the execution of so laudable a resolution we shall leave her, to follow the fortunes of the hapless victim of imprudence and evil counsellors.

Chapter XVI.

Necessary Digression

ON BOARD OF THE SHIP in which Charlotte and Mademoiselle were embarked, was an officer of large unincumbered fortune and elevated rank, and whom I shall call Crayton.

He was one of those men, who, having travelled in their youth, pretend to have contracted a peculiar fondness for every thing foreign, and to hold in contempt the productions of their own country; and this affected partiality extended even to the women.

With him therefore the blushing modesty and unaffected simplicity of Charlotte passed unnoticed; but the forward pertness of La Rue, the freedom of her conversation, the elegance of her person, mixed with a certain engaging *je ne sais quoi*, perfectly enchanted him.

The reader no doubt has already developed the character of La Rue: designing, artful, and selfish, she had accepted the devoirs[5] of Belcour because she was heartily weary of the retired life she led at the school, wished to be released from what she deemed a slavery, and to return to that vortex of folly and dissipation which had once plunged her into the deepest misery; but her plan she flattered herself was now better formed: she resolved to put herself under the protection of no man till she had first secured a settlement; but the clandestine manner in which she left Madame Du Pont's prevented her putting this plan in execution, though Belcour solemnly protested he would make her a handsome settlement the moment they arrived at Portsmouth. This he afterwards contrived to evade by a pretended hurry of business; La Rue readily conceiving he never meant to fulfil his promise, determined to change her battery, and attack the heart of Colonel Crayton. She soon discovered the partiality he entertained for her nation; and having imposed on him a feigned tale of distress, representing Belcour as a villain who had seduced her from her friends under promise of marriage, and afterwards betrayed her, pretending great remorse for the errors she had committed, and declaring whatever her affection for Belcour might have been, it was now entirely extinguished, and she wished for nothing more than an opportunity to leave a course of life which her soul abhorred; but she had no friends to apply to, they had all renounced her, and guilt and misery would undoubtedly be her future portion through life.

Crayton was possessed of many amiable qualities, though the peculiar trait in his character, which we have already mentioned, in a great measure threw a shade over them. He was beloved for his humanity and benevolence by all who knew him, but he was easy and unsuspicious himself, and became a dupe to the artifice of others.

He was, when very young, united to an amiable Parisian lady, and perhaps it was his affection for her that laid the foundation for the partiality he ever retained for the whole nation. He had by her one daughter, who entered into the world but a few hours before her mother left it. This lady was universally beloved and admired, being endowed with all the virtues of her mother, without the weakness of the father: she was married to Major Beauchamp, and was at this time in the same fleet with her father, attending her husband to New-York.

Crayton was melted by the affected contrition and distress of La Rue: he would converse with her for hours, read to her, play cards with her,

---

5. *devoirs*: Acts or expressions of civility or courtesy, signs of attentiveness to another.

listen to all her complaints, and promise to protect her to the utmost of his power. La Rue easily saw his character; her sole aim was to awaken a passion in his bosom that might turn out to her advantage, and in this aim she was but too successful, for before the voyage was finished, the infatuated Colonel gave her from under his hand a promise of marriage on their arrival at New-York, under forfeiture of five thousand pounds.

And how did our poor Charlotte pass her time during a tedious and tempestuous passage? naturally delicate, the fatigue and sickness which she endured rendered her so weak as to be almost entirely confined to her bed: yet the kindness and attention of Montraville in some measure contributed to alleviate her sufferings, and the hope of hearing from her friends soon after her arrival, kept up her spirits, and cheered many a gloomy hour.

But during the voyage a great revolution took place not only in the fortune of La Rue but in the bosom of Belcour: whilst in pursuit of his amour with Mademoiselle, he had attended little to the interesting, inobtrusive charms of Charlotte, but when, cloyed by possession, and disgusted with the art and dissimulation of one, he beheld the simplicity and gentleness of the other, the contrast became too striking not to fill him at once with surprise and admiration. He frequently conversed with Charlotte; he found her sensible, well informed, but diffident and unassuming. The languor which the fatigue of her body and perturbation of her mind spread over her delicate features, served only in his opinion to render her more lovely: he knew that Montraville did not design to marry her, and he formed a resolution to endeavour to gain her himself whenever Montraville should leave her.

Let not the reader imagine Belcour's designs were honourable. Alas! when once a woman has forgot the respect due to herself, by yielding to the solicitations of illicit love, they lose all their consequence, even in the eyes of the man whose art has betrayed them, and for whose sake they have sacrificed every valuable consideration.

> The heedless Fair, who stoops to guilty joys,
> A man may pity – but he must despise.

Nay, every libertine will think he has a right to insult her with his licentious passion; and should the unhappy creature shrink from the insolent overture, he will sneeringly taunt her with pretence of modesty.

Chapter XVII.

A Wedding

ON THE DAY BEFORE their arrival at New-York, after dinner, Crayton arose from his seat, and placing himself by Mademoiselle, thus addressed the company—

"As we are now nearly arrived at our destined port, I think it but my duty to inform you, my friends, that this lady," (taking her hand,) "has placed herself under my protection. I have seen and severely felt the anguish of her heart, and through every shade which cruelty or malice may throw over her, can discover the most amiable qualities. I thought it but necessary to mention my esteem for her before our disembarkation, as it is my fixed resolution, the morning after we land, to give her an undoubted title to my favour and protection by honourably uniting my fate to hers. I would wish every gentleman here therefore to remember that her honour henceforth is mine, and," continued he, looking at Belcour, "should any man presume to speak in the least disrespectfully of her, I shall not hesitate to pronounce him a scoundrel."

Belcour cast at him a smile of contempt, and bowing profoundly low, wished Mademoiselle much joy in the proposed union; and assuring the Colonel that he need not be in the least apprehensive of any one throwing the least odium on the character of his lady, shook him by the hand with ridiculous gravity, and left the cabin.

The truth was, he was glad to be rid of La Rue, and so he was but freed from her, he cared not who fell a victim to her infamous arts.

The inexperienced Charlotte was astonished at what she heard. She thought La Rue had, like herself, only been urged by the force of her attachment to Belcour, to quit her friends, and follow him to the seat of war: how wonderful then, that she should resolve to marry another man. It was certainly extremely wrong. It was indelicate. She mentioned her thoughts to Montraville. He laughed at her simplicity, called her a little ideot, and patting her on the cheek, said she knew nothing of the world. "If the world sanctifies such things, 'tis a very bad world I think," said Charlotte. "Why I always understood they were to have been married when they arrived at New-York. I am sure Mademoiselle told me Belcour promised to marry her."

"Well, and suppose he did?"

"Why, he should be obliged to keep his word I think."

"Well, but I suppose he has changed his mind," said Montraville, "and then you know the case is altered,"

Charlotte looked at him attentively for a moment. A full sense of her own situation rushed upon her mind. She burst into tears, and remained silent. Montraville too well understood the cause of her tears. He kissed her cheek, and bidding her not make herself uneasy, unable to bear the silent but keen remonstrance, hastily left her.

The next morning by sun-rise they found themselves at anchor before the city of New-York. A boat was ordered to convey the ladies on shore. Crayton accompanied them; and they were shewn to a house of public entertainment. Scarcely were they seated when the door opened, and the Colonel found himself in the arms of his daughter, who had landed a few minutes before him. The first transport of meeting subsided, Crayton introduced his daughter to Mademoiselle La Rue, as an old friend of her mother's, (for the artful French woman had really made it appear to the credulous Colonel that she was in the same convent with his first wife, and, though much younger, had received many tokens of her esteem and regard.)

"If, Mademoiselle," said Mrs. Beauchamp, "you were the friend of my mother, you must be worthy the esteem of all good hearts."

"Mademoiselle will soon honour our family," said Crayton, "by supplying the place that valuable woman filled: and as you are married, my dear, I think you will not blame – "

"Hush, my dear Sir," replied Mrs. Beauchamp: "I know my duty too well to scrutinize your conduct. Be assured, my dear father, your happiness is mine. I shall rejoice in it, and sincerely love the person who contributes to it. But tell me," continued she, turning to Charlotte, "who is this lovely girl? Is she your sister, Mademoiselle?"

A blush, deep as the glow of the carnation, suffused the cheeks of Charlotte.

"It is a young lady," replied the Colonel, "who came in the same vessel with us from England." He then drew his daughter aside, and told her in a whisper, Charlotte was the mistress of Montraville.

"What a pity!" said Mrs. Beauchamp softly, (casting a most compassionate glance at her.) "But surely her mind is not depraved. The goodness of her heart is depicted in her ingenuous countenance."

Charlotte caught the word pity. "And am I already fallen so low?" said she. A sigh escaped her, and a tear was ready to start, but Montraville appeared, and she checked the rising emotion. Mademoiselle went with the Colonel and his daughter to another apartment. Charlotte remained with Montraville and Belcour. The next morning the Colonel performed his promise, and La Rue became in due form Mrs. Crayton, exulted in her own good fortune, and dared to look with an eye of contempt on the unfortunate but far less guilty Charlotte.

END OF THE FIRST VOLUME.

Chapter XVIII.

Reflections

"AND AM I INDEED fallen so low," said Charlotte, "as to be only pitied? Will the voice of approbation no more meet my ear? and shall I never again possess a friend, whose face will wear a smile of joy whenever I approach? Alas! how thoughtless, how dreadfully imprudent have I been! I know not which is most painful to endure, the sneer of contempt, or the glance of compassion, which is depicted in the various countenances of my own sex: they are both equally humiliating. Ah! my dear parents, could you now see the child of your affections, the daughter whom you so dearly loved, a poor solitary being, without society, here wearing out her heavy hours in deep regret and anguish of heart, no kind friend of her own sex to whom she can unbosom her griefs, no beloved mother, no woman of character will appear in my company, and low as your Charlotte is fallen, she cannot associate with infamy."

These were the painful reflections which occupied the mind of Charlotte. Montraville had placed her in a small house a few miles from New-York: he gave her one female attendant, and supplied her with what money she wanted; but business and pleasure so entirely occupied his time, that he had little to devote to the woman, whom he had brought from all her connections, and robbed of innocence. Sometimes, indeed, he would steal out at the close of evening, and pass a few hours with her; and then so much was she attached to him, that all her sorrows were forgotten while blest with his society: she would enjoy a walk by moonlight, or sit by him in a little arbour at the bottom of the garden, and play on the harp, accompanying it with her plaintive, harmonious voice. But often, very often, did he promise to renew his visits, and, forgetful of his promise, leave her to mourn her disappointment. What painful hours of expectation would she pass! She would sit at a window which looked toward a field he used to cross, counting the minutes, and straining her eyes to catch the first glimpse of his person, till blinded with tears of disappointment, she would lean her head on her hands, and give free vent to her sorrows: then catching at some new hope, she would again renew her watchful position, till the shades of evening enveloped every object in a dusky cloud: she would then renew her complaints, and, with a heart bursting with disappointed love and wounded sensibility, retire to a bed which remorse had strewed with thorns, and court in vain that comforter of weary nature (who seldom visits the unhappy) to come and steep her senses in oblivion.

Who can form an adequate idea of the sorrow that preyed upon the mind of Charlotte? The wife, whose breast glows with affection to her husband, and who in return meets only indifference, can but faintly conceive her anguish. Dreadfully painful is the situation of such a woman, but she has many comforts of which our poor Charlotte was deprived. The duteous, faithful wife, though treated with indifference, has one solid pleasure within her own bosom, she can reflect that she has not deserved neglect – that she has ever fulfilled the duties of her station with the strictest exactness; she may hope, by constant assiduity and unremitted attention, to recall her wanderer, and be doubly happy in his returning affection; she knows he cannot leave her to unite himself to another: he cannot cast her out to poverty and contempt; she looks around her, and sees the smile of friendly welcome, or the tear of affectionate consolation, on the face of every person whom she favours with her esteem; and from all these circumstances she gathers comfort: but the poor girl by thoughtless passion led astray, who, in parting with her honour, has forfeited the esteem of the very man to whom she has sacrificed every thing dear and valuable in life, feels his indifference in the fruit of her own folly, and laments her want of power to recall his lost affection; she knows there is no tie but honour, and that, in a man who has been guilty of seduction, is but very feeble: he may leave her in a moment to shame and want; he may marry and forsake her for ever; and should he, she has no redress, no friendly, soothing companion to pour into her wounded mind the balm of consolation, no benevolent hand to lead her back to the path of rectitude; she has disgraced her friends, forfeited the good opinion of the world, and undone herself; she feels herself a poor solitary being in the midst of surrounding multitudes; shame bows her to the earth, remorse tears her distracted mind, and guilt, poverty, and disease close the dreadful scene: she sinks unnoticed to oblivion. The finger of contempt may point out to some passing daughter of youthful mirth, the humble bed where lies this frail sister of mortality; and will she, in the unbounded gaiety of her heart, exult in her own unblemished fame, and triumph over the silent ashes of the dead? Oh no! has she a heart of sensibility, she will stop, and thus address the unhappy victim of folly –

"Thou had'st thy faults, but sure thy sufferings have expiated them: thy errors brought thee to an early grave; but thou wert a fellow-creature – thou hast been unhappy – then be those errors forgotten."

Then, as she stoops to pluck the noxious weed from off the sod, a tear will fall, and consecrate the spot to Charity.

For ever honoured be the sacred drop of humanity; the angel of mercy shall record its source, and the soul from whence it sprang shall be immortal.

My dear Madam, contract not your brow into a frown of disapprobation. I mean not to extenuate the faults of those unhappy women who fall victims to guilt and folly; but surely, when we reflect how many errors we are ourselves subject to, how many secret faults lie hid in the recesses of our hearts, which we should blush to have brought into open day (and yet those faults require the lenity and pity of a benevolent judge, or awful would be our prospect of futurity) I say, my dear Madam, when we consider this, we surely may pity the faults of others.

Believe me, many an unfortunate female, who has once strayed into the thorny paths of vice, would gladly return to virtue, was any generous friend to endeavour to raise and re-assure her; but alas! it cannot be, you say; the world would deride and scoff. Then let me tell you, Madam, 'tis a very unfeeling world and does not deserve half the blessings which a bountiful Providence showers upon it.

Oh, thou benevolent giver of all good! how shall we erring mortals dare to look up to thy mercy in the great day of retribution, if we now uncharitably refuse to overlook the errors, or alleviate the miseries, of our fellow-creatures.

Chapter XIX.

A Mistake Discovered

JULIA FRANKLIN WAS the only child of a man of large property, who, at the age of eighteen, left her independent mistress of an unincumbered income of seven hundred a year; she was a girl of a lively disposition, and humane, susceptible heart: she resided in New-York with an uncle, who loved her too well, and had too high an opinion of her prudence, to scrutinize her actions so much as would have been necessary with many young ladies, who were not blest with her discretion: she was, at the time Montraville arrived at New-York, the life of society, and the universal toast. Montraville was introduced to her by the following accident.

One night when he was upon guard, a dreadful fire broke out near Mr. Franklin's house, which, in a few hours, reduced that and several others to ashes; fortunately no lives were lost, and, by the assiduity of the soldiers, much valuable property was saved from the flames. In the midst of the confusion an old gentleman came up to Montraville, and, putting a small box into his hands, cried—"Keep it, my good Sir, till I come to you again;" and then rushing again into the thickest of the croud, Montraville saw him no more. He waited till the fire was quite extinguished and the mob dispersed; but in vain: the old gentleman did not appear to claim his property; and Montraville, fearing to make any enquiry, lest he should meet with impostors who might lay claim, without any legal right, to the box, carried it to his lodgings, and locked it up: he naturally imagined, that the person who committed it to his care knew him, and would, in a day or two, reclaim it; but several weeks passed on, and no enquiry being made, he began to be uneasy, and resolved to examine the contents of the box, and if they were, as he supposed, valuable, to spare no pains to discover, and restore them to the owner. Upon opening it, he found it contained jewels to a large amount, about two hundred pounds in money, and a miniature picture set for a bracelet. On examining the picture, he thought he had somewhere seen features very like it, but could not recollect where. A few days after, being at a public assembly, he saw Miss Franklin, and the likeness was too evident to be mistaken: he enquired among his brother officers if any of them knew her, and found one who was upon terms of intimacy in the family: "then introduce me to her immediately," said he, "for I am certain I can inform her of something which will give her peculiar pleasure."

He was immediately introduced, found she was the owner of the jewels, and was invited to breakfast the next morning in order to their restoration. This whole evening Montraville was honoured with Julia's hand; the lively sallies of her wit, the elegance of her manner, powerfully charmed him: he forgot Charlotte, and indulged himself in saying every thing that was polite and tender to Julia. But on retiring, recollection returned. "What am I about?" said he: "though I cannot marry Charlotte, I cannot be villain enough to forsake her, nor must I dare to trifle with the heart of Julia Franklin. I will return this box," said he, "which has been the source of so much uneasiness already, and in the evening pay a visit to my poor melancholy Charlotte, and endeavour to forget this fascinating Julia."

He arose, dressed himself, and taking the picture out, "I will reserve this from the rest," said he, "and by presenting it to her when she thinks it is lost, enhance the value of the obligation." He repaired to Mr. Franklin's, and found Julia in the breakfast parlour alone.

"How happy am I, Madam," said he, "that being the fortunate instrument of saving these jewels has been the means of procuring me the acquaintance of so amiable a lady. There are the jewels and money all safe."

"But where is the picture, Sir?" said Julia.

"Here, Madam. I would not willingly part with it."

"It is the portrait of my mother," said she, taking it from him: "'tis all that remains." She pressed it to her lips, and a tear trembled in her eyes. Montraville glanced his eye on her grey night gown and black ribbon, and his own feelings prevented a reply.

Julia Franklin was the very reverse of Charlotte Temple: she was tall, elegantly shaped, and possessed much of the air and manner of a woman of fashion; her complexion was a clear brown, enlivened with the glow of health, her eyes, full, black, and sparkling, darted their intelligent glances through long silken lashes; her hair was shining brown, and her features regular and striking; there was an air of innocent gaiety that played about her countenance, where good humour sat triumphant.

"I have been mistaken," said Montraville. "I imagined I loved Charlotte: but alas! I am now too late convinced my attachment to her was merely the impulse of the moment. I fear I have not only entailed lasting misery on that poor girl, but also thrown a barrier in the way of my own happiness, which it will be impossible to surmount. I feel I love Julia Franklin with ardour and sincerity; yet, when in her presence, I am sensible of my own inability to offer a heart worthy her acceptance, and remain silent."

Full of these painful thoughts, Montraville walked out to see Charlotte: she saw him approach, and ran out to meet him: she banished from her countenance the air of discontent which ever appeared when he was absent, and met him with a smile of joy.

"I thought you had forgot me, Montraville," said she, "and was very unhappy."

"I shall never forget you, Charlotte," he replied, pressing her hand.

The uncommon gravity of his countenance, and the brevity of his reply, alarmed her.

"You are not well," said she; "your hand is hot; your eyes are heavy; you are very ill."

"I am a villain," said he mentally, as he turned from her to hide his emotions.

"But come," continued she tenderly, "you shall go to bed, and I will sit by, and watch you; you will be better when you have slept."

Montraville was glad to retire, and by pretending sleep, hide the agitation of his mind from her penetrating eye. Charlotte watched by him till a late hour, and then, lying softly down by his side, sunk into a profound sleep, from whence she awoke not till late the next morning.

Chapter XX.

Virtue never appears so amiable as when reaching forth her hand
to raise a fallen sister.

Chapter of Accidents.

WHEN CHARLOTTE AWOKE, she missed Montraville; but thinking he might have arisen early to enjoy the beauties of the morning, she was preparing to follow him, when casting her eye on the table, she saw a note, and opening it hastily, found these words –

"My dear Charlotte must not be surprised, if she does not see me again for some time: unavoidable business will prevent me that pleasure: be assured I am quite well this morning; and what your fond imagination magnified into illness, was nothing more than fatigue, which a few hours rest has entirely removed. Make yourself happy, and be certain of the unalterable friendship of

MONTRAVILLE."

"*Friendship!*" said Charlotte emphatically, as she finished the note, "is it come to this at last? Alas! poor, forsaken Charlotte, thy doom is now but too apparent. Montraville is no longer interested in thy happiness; and shame, remorse, and disappointed love will henceforth be thy only attendants."

Though these were the ideas that involuntarily rushed upon the mind of Charlotte as she perused the fatal note, yet after a few hours had elapsed, the syren[6] Hope again took possession of her bosom, and she flat-

6. *sirens*: In Greek mythology, the sirens were sea nymphs who lured sailors with seductive singing to death on the rocks surrounding their island.

tered herself she could, on a second perusal, discover an air of tenderness in the few lines he had left, which at first had escaped her notice.

"He certainly cannot be so base as to leave me," said she, "and in stiling himself my friend does he not promise to protect me. I will not torment myself with these causeless fears; I will place a confidence in his honour; and sure he will not be so unjust as to abuse it."

Just as she had by this manner of reasoning brought her mind to some tolerable degree of composure, she was surprised by a visit from Belcour. The dejection visible in Charlotte's countenance, her swoln eyes and neglected attire, at once told him she was unhappy: he made no doubt but Montraville had, by his coldness, alarmed her suspicions, and was resolved, if possible, to rouse her to jealousy, urge her to reproach him, and by that means occasion a breach between them. "If I can once convince her that she has a rival," said he, "she will listen to my passion if it is only to revenge his slights." Belcour knew but little of the female heart; and what he did know was only of those of loose and dissolute lives. He had no idea that a woman might fall a victim to imprudence, and yet retain so strong a sense of honour, as to reject with horror and contempt every solicitation to a second fault. He never imagined that a gentle, generous female heart, once tenderly attached, when treated with unkindness might break, but would never harbour a thought of revenge.

His visit was not long, but before he went he fixed a scorpion in the heart of Charlotte, whose venom embittered every future hour of her life.

We will now return for a moment to Colonel Crayton. He had been three months married, and in that little time had discovered that the conduct of his lady was not so prudent as it ought to have been: but remonstrance was vain; her temper was violent; and to the Colonel's great misfortune he had conceived a sincere affection for her: she saw her own power, and, with the art of a Circe[7] made every action appear to him in what light she pleased: his acquaintance laughed at his blindness, his friends pitied his infatuation, his amiable daughter, Mrs. Beauchamp, in secret deplored the loss of her father's affection, and grieved that he should be so entirely swayed by an artful, and, she much feared, infamous woman.

Mrs. Beauchamp was mild and engaging; she loved not the hurry and bustle of a city, and had prevailed on her husband to take a house a few miles from New-York. Chance led her into the same neighbourhood with Charlotte; their houses stood within a short space of each other, and their gardens joined: she had not been long in her new habitation before the

7. *Circe*: In Greek mythology, Circe is a magician or enchanter. She is the character in the *Odyssey* who kept Odysseus with her for a year and turned his men into swine.

figure of Charlotte struck her; she recollected her interesting features; she saw the melancholy so conspicuous in her countenance, and her heart bled at the reflection, that perhaps deprived of honour, friends, all that was valuable in life, she was doomed to linger out a wretched existence in a strange land, and sink brokenhearted into an untimely grave. "Would to heaven I could snatch her from so hard a fate," said she; "but the merciless world has barred the doors of compassion against a poor weak girl, who, perhaps, had she one kind friend to raise and reassure her, would gladly return to peace and virtue; nay, even the woman who dares to pity, and endeavour to recall a wandering sister, incurs the sneer of contempt and ridicule, for an action in which even angels are said to rejoice."

The longer Mrs. Beauchamp was a witness to the solitary life Charlotte led, the more she wished to speak to her, and often as she saw her cheeks wet with the tears of anguish, she would say – "Dear sufferer, how gladly would I pour into your heart the balm of consolation, were it not for the fear of derision."

But an accident soon happened which made her resolve to brave even the scoffs of the world, rather than not enjoy the heavenly satisfaction of comforting a desponding fellow-creature.

Mrs. Beauchamp was an early riser. She was one morning walking in the garden, leaning on her husband's arm, when the sound of a harp attracted their notice: they listened attentively, and heard a soft melodious voice distinctly sing the following stanzas:

> Thou glorious orb, supremely bright,
> Just rising from the sea,
>   To chear all nature with thy light,
> What are thy beams to me?
>   In vain thy glories bid me rise,
> To hail the new-born day,
>   Alas! my morning sacrifice
> Is still to weep and pray.
>   For what are nature's charms combin'd,
> To one, whose weary breast
>   Can neither peace nor comfort find,
> Nor friend whereon to rest?
>   Oh! never! never! whilst I live
> Can my heart's anguish cease:
>   Come, friendly death, thy mandate give,
> And let me be at peace.

" 'Tis poor Charlotte!" said Mrs. Beauchamp, the pellucid drop of humanity stealing down her cheek.

Captain Beauchamp was alarmed at her emotion. "What Charlotte?" said he; "do you know her?"

In the accent of a pitying angel did she disclose to her husband Charlotte's unhappy situation, and the frequent wish she had formed of being serviceable to her. "I fear," continued she, "the poor girl has been basely betrayed; and if I thought you would not blame me, I would pay her a visit, offer her my friendship, and endeavour to restore to her heart that peace she seems to have lost, and so pathetically laments. Who knows, my dear," laying her hand affectionately on his arm, "who knows but she has left some kind, affectionate parents to lament her errors, and would she return, they might with rapture receive the poor penitent, and wash away her faults in tears of joy. Oh! what a glorious reflexion would it be for me could I be the happy instrument of restoring her. Her heart may not be depraved, Beauchamp."

"Exalted woman!" cried Beauchamp, embracing her, "how dost thou rise every moment in my esteem. Follow the impulse of thy generous heart, my Emily. Let prudes and fools censure if they dare, and blame a sensibility they never felt; I will exultingly tell them that the heart that is truly virtuous is ever inclined to pity and forgive the errors of its fellow-creatures."

A beam of exulting joy played round the animated countenance of Mrs. Beauchamp, at these encomiums bestowed on her by a beloved husband, the most delightful sensations pervaded her heart, and, having breakfasted, she prepared to visit Charlotte.

Chapter XXI.

Teach me to feel another's woe,
   To hide the fault I see,
That mercy I to others show,
   That mercy show to me.

Pope.[8]

WHEN MRS. BEAUCHAMP was dressed, she began to feel embarrassed at the thought of beginning an acquaintance with Charlotte, and was distressed how to make the first visit. "I cannot go without some introduction," said

8. These lines are from Alexander Pope (1688-1744), "The Universal Prayer."

she, "it will look so like impertinent curiosity." At length recollecting herself, she stepped into the garden, and gathering a few fine cucumbers, took them in her hand by way of apology for her visit.

A glow of conscious shame vermillioned Charlotte's face as Mrs. Beauchamp entered.

"You will pardon me, Madam," said she, "for not having before paid my respects to so amiable a neighbour; but we English people always keep up that reserve which is the characteristic of our nation wherever we go. I have taken the liberty to bring you a few cucumbers, for I observed you had none in your garden."

Charlotte, though naturally polite and well-bred, was so confused she could hardly speak. Her kind visitor endeavoured to relieve her by not noticing her embarrassment. "I am come, Madam," continued she, "to request you will spend the day with me. I shall be alone; and, as we are both strangers in this country, we may hereafter be extremely happy in each other's friendship."

"Your friendship, Madam," said Charlotte blushing, "is an honour to all who are favoured with it. Little as I have seen of this part of the world, I am no stranger to Mrs. Beauchamp's goodness of heart and known humanity: but my friendship – " She paused, glanced her eye upon her own visible situation, and, spite of her endeavours to suppress them, burst into tears.

Mrs. Beauchamp guessed the source from whence those tears flowed. "You seem unhappy, Madam," said she: "shall I be thought worthy your confidence? will you entrust me with the cause of your sorrow, and rest on my assurances to exert my utmost power to serve you." Charlotte returned a look of gratitude, but could not speak, and Mrs. Beauchamp continued – "My heart was interested in your behalf the first moment I saw you, and I only lament I had not made earlier overtures towards an acquaintance; but I flatter myself you will henceforth consider me as your friend."

"Oh Madam!" cried Charlotte, "I have forfeited the good opinion of all my friends; I have forsaken them, and undone myself."

"Come, come, my dear," said Mrs. Beauchamp, "you must not indulge these gloomy thoughts: you are not I hope so miserable as you imagine yourself: endeavour to be composed, and let me be favoured with your company at dinner, when, if you can bring yourself to think me your friend, and repose a confidence in me, I am ready to convince you it shall not be abused." She then arose, and bade her good morning.

At the dining hour Charlotte repaired to Mrs. Beauchamp's, and during dinner assumed as composed an aspect as possible; but when the cloth was removed, she summoned all her resolution and determined to make Mrs. Beauchamp acquainted with every circumstance preceding her unfortunate elopement, and the earnest desire she had to quit a way of life so repugnant to her feelings.

With the benignant aspect of an angel of mercy did Mrs. Beauchamp listen to the artless tale: she was shocked to the soul to find how large a share La Rue had in the seduction of this amiable girl, and a tear fell, when she reflected so vile a woman was now the wife of her father. When Charlotte had finished, she gave her a little time to collect her scattered spirits, and then asked her if she had never written to her friends.

"Oh yes, Madam," said she, "frequently: but I have broke their hearts: they are either dead or have cast me off for ever, for I have never received a single line from them."

"I rather suspect," said Mrs. Beauchamp, "they have never had your letters: but suppose you were to hear from them, and they were willing to receive you, would you then leave this cruel Montraville, and return to them?"

"Would I!" said Charlotte, clasping her hands; "would not the poor sailor, tost on a tempestuous ocean, threatened every moment with death, gladly return to the shore he had left to trust to its deceitful calmness? Oh, my dear Madam, I would return, though to do it I were obliged to walk barefoot over a burning desart, and beg a scanty pittance of each traveller to support my existence. I would endure it all chearfully, could I but once more see my dear, blessed mother, hear her pronounce my pardon, and bless me before I died; but alas! I shall never see her more; she has blotted the ungrateful Charlotte from her remembrance, and I shall sink to the grave loaded with her's and my father's curse."

Mrs. Beauchamp endeavoured to sooth her. "You shall write to them again," said she, "and I will see that the letter is sent by the first packet that sails for England; in the mean time keep up your spirits, and hope every thing, by daring to deserve it."

She then turned the conversation, and Charlotte having taken a cup of tea, wished her benevolent friend a good evening.

Chapter XXII.

Sorrows of the Heart

WHEN CHARLOTTE got home she endeavoured to collect her thoughts, and took up a pen in order to address those dear parents, whom, spite of her errors, she still loved with the utmost tenderness, but vain was every effort to write with the least coherence; her tears fell so fast they almost blinded her; and as she proceeded to describe her unhappy situation, she became so agitated that she was obliged to give over the attempt and retire to bed, where, overcome with the fatigue her mind had undergone, she fell into a slumber which greatly refreshed her, and she arose in the morning with spirits more adequate to the painful task she had to perform, and, after several attempts, at length concluded the following letter to her mother—

To Mrs. Temple.

New-York.

"Will my once kind, my ever beloved mother, deign to receive a letter from her guilty, but repentant child? or has she, justly incensed at my ingratitude, driven the unhappy Charlotte from her remembrance? Alas! thou much injured mother! shouldst thou even disown me, I dare not complain, because I know I have deserved it: but yet, believe me, guilty as I am, and cruelly as I have disappointed the hopes of the fondest parents, that ever girl had, even in the moment when, forgetful of my duty, I fled from you and happiness, even then I loved you most, and my heart bled at the thought of what you would suffer. Oh! never, never! whilst I have existence, will the agony of that moment be erased from my memory. It seemed like the separation of soul and body. What can I plead in excuse for my conduct? alas! nothing! That I loved my seducer is but too true! yet powerful as that passion is when operating in a young heart glowing with sensibility, it never would have conquered my affection to you, my beloved parents, had I not been encouraged, nay, urged to take the fatally imprudent step, by one of my own sex, who, under the mask of friendship, drew me on to ruin. Yet think not your Charlotte was so lost as to voluntarily rush into a life of infamy; no, my dear mother, deceived by the specious appearance of my betrayer, and every suspicion lulled asleep by the most solemn promises of marriage, I thought not those promises would so easily be forgotten. I never once reflected that the man who could stoop to seduction, would not hesitate to forsake the wretched object of his passion, whenever his capricious heart grew weary of her tenderness. When we arrived at this place, I vainly expected him to fulfil his engagements, but was at last fatally convinced he had never intended to make me his wife, or if he had once thought of it, his mind was now altered. I scorned to claim from his humanity what I could not obtain from his love: I was conscious of having forfeited the only gem that could render me respectable in the eye of the world. I locked my sorrows in my own bosom, and bore my injuries in silence. But how shall I proceed? This man, this cruel Montraville, for whom I sacrificed honour, happiness, and the love of my friends, no longer looks on me with affection, but scorns the credulous girl whom his art has made miserable. Could you see me, my dear parents, without society, without friends, stung with remorse, and (I feel the burning blush of shame die my cheeks while I write it) tortured with the pangs of disappointed love; cut to the soul by the indifference of him, who, having deprived me of every other comfort, no longer thinks it worth his while to sooth the heart where he has planted the thorn of never-ceasing regret. My daily employment is to think of you and weep, to pray for your happiness and deplore my own folly: my nights are scarce more happy, for if by chance I close my weary eyes, and hope some small forgetfulness of sorrow, some little time to pass in sweet oblivion, fancy, still waking, wafts me home to you: I see your beloved forms, I kneel and hear the blessed words of peace and pardon. Extatic joy pervades my soul; I reach my arms to catch your dear embraces; the motion chases the illusive dream; I wake to real misery. At other times I see my father angry and frowning, point to horrid caves, where, on the cold damp ground, in the agonies of death, I see my dear mother and my revered grand-father. I strive to raise you; you push me from you, and shrieking cry – "Charlotte, thou hast murdered me!" Horror and despair tear every tortured nerve; I start, and leave my restless bed, weary and unrefreshed.

"Shocking as these reflexions are, I have yet one more dreadful than the rest. Mother, my dear mother! do not let me quite break your heart when I tell you, in a few months I shall bring into the world an innocent witness of my guilt. Oh my bleeding heart, I shall bring a poor little helpless creature, heir to infamy and shame.

"This alone has urged me once more to address you, to interest you in behalf of this poor unborn, and beg you to extend your protection to the child of your lost Charlotte; for my own part I have wrote so often, so frequently have pleaded for forgiveness, and entreated to be received once more beneath the paternal roof, that having received no answer, not even one line, I much fear you have cast me from you for ever.

"But sure you cannot refuse to protect my innocent infant: it partakes not of its mother's guilt. Oh my father, oh beloved mother, now do I feel the anguish I inflicted on your hearts recoiling with double force upon my own.

"If my child should be a girl (which heaven forbid) tell her the unhappy fate of her mother, and teach her to avoid my errors; if a boy, teach him to lament my miseries, but tell him not who inflicted them, lest in wishing to revenge his mother's injuries, he should wound the peace of his father.

"And now, dear friends of my soul, kind guardians of my infancy, farewell. I feel I never more must hope to see you; the anguish of my heart strikes at the strings of life, and in a short time I shall be at rest. Oh could I but receive your blessing and forgiveness before I died, it would smooth my passage to the peaceful grave, and be a blessed foretaste of a happy eternity. I beseech you, curse me not, my adored parents, but let a tear of pity and pardon fall to the memory of your lost   CHARLOTTE."

Chapter XXIII.

A Man May Smile, and Smile, and Be a Villain

WHILE CHARLOTTE was enjoying some small degree of comfort in the consoling friendship of Mrs. Beauchamp, Montraville was advancing rapidly in his affection towards Miss Franklin. Julia was an amiable girl; she saw only the fair side of his character; she possessed an independent fortune, and resolved to be happy with the man of her heart, though his rank and fortune were by no means so exalted as she had a right to expect; she saw the passion which Montraville struggled to conceal; she wondered at his timidity, but imagined the distance fortune had placed between them occasioned his backwardness, and made every advance which strict prudence and a becoming modesty would permit. Montraville saw with pleasure he was not indifferent to her, but a spark of honour which animated his bosom would not suffer him to take advantage of her partiality. He was well acquainted with Charlotte's situation, and he thought there would be a double cruelty in forsaking her at such a time; and to marry Miss Franklin, while honour, humanity, every sacred law, obliged him still to protect and support Charlotte, was a baseness which his soul shuddered at.

He communicated his uneasiness to Belcour: it was the very thing this pretended friend had wished. "And do you really," said he, laughing, "hesitate at marrying the lovely Julia, and becoming master of her fortune, because a little foolish, fond girl chose to leave her friends, and run away with you to America. Dear Montraville, act more like a man of sense; this whining, pining Charlotte, who occasions you so much uneasiness, would have eloped with somebody else if she had not with you."

"Would to heaven," said Montraville, "I had never seen her; my regard for her was but the momentary passion of desire, but I feel I shall love and revere Julia Franklin as long as I live; yet to leave poor Charlotte in her present situation would be cruel beyond description."

"Oh my good sentimental friend," said Belcour, "do you imagine no body has a right to provide for the brat but yourself."

Montraville started. "Sure," said he, "you cannot mean to insinuate that Charlotte is false."

"I don't insinuate it," said Belcour, "I know it."

Montraville turned pale as ashes. "Then there is no faith in woman," said he.

"While I thought you attached to her," said Belcour with an air of indifference, "I never wished to make you uneasy by mentioning her perfidy, but as I know you love and are beloved by Miss Franklin, I was determined not to let these foolish scruples of honour step between you and happiness, or your tenderness for the peace of a perfidious girl prevent your uniting yourself to a woman of honour."

"Good heavens!" said Montraville, "what poignant reflections does a man endure who sees a lovely woman plunged in infamy, and is conscious he was her first seducer; but are you certain of what you say, Belcour?"

"So far," replied he, "that I myself have received advances from her which I would not take advantage of out of regard to you: but hang it, think no more about her. I dined at Franklin's to-day, and Julia bid me seek and bring you to tea: so come along, my lad, make good use of opportunity, and seize the gifts of fortune while they are within your reach."

Montraville was too much agitated to pass a happy evening even in the company of Julia Franklin: he determined to visit Charlotte early the next morning, tax her with her falsehood, and take an everlasting leave of her; but when the morning came, he was commanded on duty, and for six weeks was prevented from putting his design in execution. At length he found an hour to spare, and walked out to spend it with Charlotte: it was near four o'clock in the afternoon when he arrived at her cottage; she was not in the parlour, and without calling the servant he walked up stairs, thinking to find her in her bed room. He opened the door, and the first object that met his eyes was Charlotte asleep on the bed, and Belcour by her side.

"Death and distraction," said he, stamping, "this is too much. Rise, villain, and defend yourself." Belcour sprang from the bed. The noise awoke Charlotte; terrified at the furious appearance of Montraville, and seeing Belcour with him in the chamber, she caught hold of his arm as he stood by the bed-side, and eagerly asked what was the matter.

"Treacherous, infamous girl," said he, "can you ask? How came he here?" pointing to Belcour.

"As heaven is my witness," replied she weeping, "I do not know. I have not seen him for these three weeks."

"Then you confess he sometimes visits you?"

"He came sometimes by your desire."

" 'Tis false; I never desired him to come, and you know I did not: but mark me, Charlotte, from this instant our connexion is at an end. Let Belcour, or any other of your favoured lovers, take you and provide for you; I have done with you for ever."

He was then going to leave her; but starting wildly from the bed, she threw herself on her knees before him, protesting her innocence and entreating him not to leave her. "Oh Montraville," said she, "kill me, for pity's sake kill me, but do not doubt my fidelity. Do not leave me in this horrid situation; for the sake of your unborn child, oh! spurn not the wretched mother from you."

"Charlotte," said he, with a firm voice, "I shall take care that neither you nor your child want any thing in the approaching painful hour; but we meet no more." He then endeavoured to raise her from the ground; but in vain; she clung about his knees, entreating him to believe her innocent, and conjuring Belcour to clear up the dreadful mystery.

Belcour cast on Montraville a smile of contempt: it irritated him almost to madness; he broke from the feeble arms of the distressed girl; she shrieked and fell prostrate on the floor.

Montraville instantly left the house and returned hastily to the city.

Chapter XXIV.

Mystery Developed

UNFORTUNATELY FOR CHARLOTTE, about three weeks before this unhappy rencontre, Captain Beauchamp, being ordered to Rhode-Island, his lady had accompanied him, so that Charlotte was deprived of her friendly advice and consoling society. The afternoon on which Montraville had visited her she had found herself languid and fatigued, and after making a very slight dinner had lain down to endeavour to recruit her exhausted spirits, and, contrary to her expectations, had fallen asleep. She had not long been lain down, when Belcour arrived, for he took every opportunity of visiting her, and striving to awaken her resentment against Montraville. He enquired of the servant where her mistress was, and being told she was asleep, took up a book to amuse himself: having sat a few minutes, he by chance cast his eyes towards the road, and saw Montraville approaching; he instantly conceived the diabolical scheme of ruining the unhappy Charlotte in his opinion for ever; he therefore stole softly up stairs, and laying himself by her side with the greatest precaution, for fear she should awake, was in that situation discovered by his credulous friend.

When Montraville spurned the weeping Charlotte from him, and left her almost distracted with terror and despair, Belcour raised her from the floor, and leading her down stairs, assumed the part of a tender, consoling friend; she listened to the arguments he advanced with apparent composure; but this was only the calm of a moment: the remembrance of Montraville's recent cruelty again rushed upon her mind: she pushed him from her with some violence, and crying—"Leave me, Sir, I beseech you leave me, for much I fear you have been the cause of my fidelity being suspected; go, leave me to the accumulated miseries my own imprudence has brought upon me."

She then left him with precipitation, and retiring to her own apartment, threw herself on the bed, and gave vent to an agony of grief which it is impossible to describe.

It now occurred to Belcour that she might possibly write to Montraville, and endeavour to convince him of her innocence: he was well aware of her pathetic remonstrances, and, sensible of the tenderness of Montraville's heart, resolved to prevent any letters ever reaching him: he therefore called the servant, and, by the powerful persuasion of a bribe, prevailed with her to promise whatever letters her mistress might write should be sent to him. He then left a polite, tender note for Charlotte, and returned to New-York. His first business was to seek Montraville, and endeavour to convince him that what had happened would ultimately tend to his happiness: he found him in his apartment, solitary, pensive, and wrapped in disagreeable reflexions.

"Why how now, whining, pining lover?" said he, clapping him on the shoulder. Montraville started; a momentary flush of resentment crossed his cheek, but instantly gave place to a death-like paleness, occasioned by painful remembrance – remembrance awakened by that monitor, whom, though we may in vain endeavour, we can never entirely silence.

"Belcour," said he, "you have injured me in a tender point."

"Prithee, Jack," replied Belcour, "do not make a serious matter of it: how could I refuse the girl's advances? and thank heaven she is not your wife."

"True," said Montraville; "but she was innocent when I first knew her. It was I seduced her, Belcour. Had it not been for me, she had still been virtuous and happy in the affection and protection of her family."

"Pshaw," replied Belcour, laughing, "if you had not taken advantage of her easy nature, some other would, and where is the difference, pray?"

"I wish I had never seen her," cried he passionately, and starting from his seat. "Oh that cursed French woman," added he with vehemence, "had it not been for her, I might have been happy – " He paused.

"With Julia Franklin," said Belcour. The name, like a sudden spark of electric fire, seemed for a moment to suspend his faculties – for a moment he was transfixed; but recovering, he caught Belcour's hand, and cried – "Stop! stop! I beseech you, name not the lovely Julia and the wretched Montraville in the same breath. I am a seducer, a mean, ungenerous seducer of unsuspecting innocence. I dare not hope that purity like her's would stoop to unite itself with black, premeditated guilt: yet by heavens I swear, Belcour, I thought I loved the lost, abandoned Charlotte till I saw Julia – I thought I never could forsake her; but the heart is deceitful, and I now can plainly discriminate between the impulse of a youthful passion, and the pure flame of disinterested affection."

At that instant Julia Franklin passed the window, leaning on her uncle's arm. She curtseyed as she passed, and, with the bewitching smile of modest chearfulness, cried – "Do you bury yourselves in the house this fine evening, gents?" There was something in the voice! the manner! the look! that was altogether irresistible. "Perhaps she wishes my company," said Montraville mentally, as he snatched up his hat: "if I thought she loved me, I would confess my errors, and trust to her generosity to pity and pardon me." He soon overtook her, and offering her his arm, they sauntered to pleasant but unfrequented walks. Belcour drew Mr. Franklin on one side and entered into a political discourse: they walked faster than the young people, and Belcour by some means contrived entirely to lose sight of them. It was a fine evening in the beginning of autumn; the last remains of day-light faintly streaked the western sky, while the moon, with pale and virgin lustre in the room of gorgeous gold and purple, ornamented the canopy of heaven with silver, fleecy clouds, which now and then half hid her lovely face, and, by partly concealing, heightened every beauty; the zephyrs whispered softly through the trees, which now began to shed their leafy honours; a solemn silence reigned: and to a happy mind an evening such as this would give serenity, and calm, unruffled pleasure; but to Montraville, while it soothed the turbulence of his passions, it brought increase of melancholy reflections. Julia was leaning on his arm: he took her hand in his, and pressing it tenderly, sighed deeply, but continued silent. Julia was embarrassed; she wished to break a silence so unaccountable, but was unable; she loved Montraville, she saw he was unhappy, and wished to know the cause of his uneasiness, but that innate modesty, which nature has implanted in the female breast, prevented her enquiring. "I am bad company, Miss Franklin," said he, at last recollecting himself; "but I have met with something to-day that has greatly distressed me, and I cannot shake off the disagreeable impression it has made on my mind."

"I am sorry," she replied, "that you have any cause of inquietude. I am sure if you were as happy as you deserve, and as all your friends wish you –" She hesitated. "And might I," replied he with some animation, "presume to rank the amiable Julia in that number?"

"Certainly," said she, "the service you have rendered me, the knowledge of your worth, all combine to make me esteem you."

"Esteem, my lovely Julia," said he passionately, "is but a poor cold word. I would if I dared, if I thought I merited your attention – but no, I must not – honour forbids. I am beneath your notice, Julia, I am miserable and cannot hope to be otherwise."

"Alas!" said Julia, "I pity you."

"Oh thou condescending charmer," said he, "how that sweet word chears my sad heart. Indeed if you knew all, you would pity; but at the same time I fear you would despise me."

Just then they were again joined by Mr. Franklin and Belcour. It had interrupted an interesting discourse. They found it impossible to converse on indifferent subjects, and proceeded home in silence. At Mr. Franklin's door Montraville again pressed Julia's hand, and faintly articulating "good night," retired to his lodgings dispirited and wretched, from a consciousness that he deserved not the affection, with which he plainly saw he was honoured.

Chapter XXV.

Reception of a Letter

"AND WHERE NOW is our poor Charlotte?" said Mr. Temple one evening, as the cold blasts of autumn whistled rudely over the heath, and the yellow appearance of the distant wood, spoke the near approach of winter. In vain the chearful fire blazed on the hearth, in vain was he surrounded by all the comforts of life; the parent was still alive in his heart, and when he thought that perhaps his once darling child was ere this exposed to all the miseries of want in a distant land, without a friend to sooth and comfort her, without the benignant look of compassion to chear, or the angelic voice of pity to pour the balm of consolation on her wounded heart; when he thought of this, his whole soul dissolved in tenderness; and while he wiped the tear of anguish from the eye of his patient, uncomplaining Lucy, he struggled to suppress the sympathizing drop that started in his own.

"Oh, my poor girl," said Mrs. Temple, "how must she be altered, else surely she would have relieved our agonizing minds by one line to say she lived – to say she had not quite forgot the parents who almost idolized her."

"Gracious heaven," said Mr. Temple, starting from his seat, "who would wish to be a father, to experience the agonizing pangs inflicted on a parent's heart by the ingratitude of a child?" Mrs. Temple wept: her father took her hand; he would have said, "be comforted my child," but the words died on his tongue. The sad silence that ensued was interrupted by a loud rap at the door. In a moment a servant entered with a letter in his hand.

Mrs. Temple took it from him: she cast her eyes upon the superscription; she knew the writing. "'Tis Charlotte," said she, eagerly breaking the seal, "she has not quite forgot us." But before she had half gone through the contents, a sudden sickness seized her; she grew cold and giddy, and putting it into her husband's hand, she cried — "Read it: I cannot." Mr. Temple attempted to read it aloud, but frequently paused to give vent to his tears. "My poor deluded child," said he, when he had finished.

"Oh, shall we not forgive the dear penitent?" said Mrs. Temple. "We must, we will, my love; she is willing to return, and 'tis our duty to receive her."

"Father of mercy," said Mr. Eldridge, raising his clasped hands, "let me but live once more to see the dear wanderer restored to her afflicted parents, and take me from this world of sorrow whenever it seemeth best to thy wisdom."

"Yes, we will receive her," said Mr. Temple; "we will endeavour to heal her wounded spirit, and speak peace and comfort to her agitated soul. I will write to her to return immediately."

"Oh!" said Mrs. Temple, "I would if possible fly to her, support and chear the dear sufferer in the approaching hour of distress, and tell her how nearly penitence is allied to virtue. Cannot we go and conduct her home, my love?" continued she, laying her hand on his arm. "My father will surely forgive our absence if we go to bring home his darling."

"You cannot go, my Lucy," said Mr. Temple: "the delicacy of your frame would but poorly sustain the fatigue of a long voyage; but I will go and bring the gentle penitent to your arms: we may still see many years of happiness."

The struggle in the bosom of Mrs. Temple between maternal and conjugal tenderness was long and painful. At length the former triumphed, and she consented that her husband should set forward to New-York by the first opportunity: she wrote to her Charlotte in the tenderest, most consoling manner, and looked forward to the happy hour, when she should again embrace her, with the most animated hope.

Chapter XXVI.

What Might Be Expected

IN THE MEAN TIME the passion Montraville had conceived for Julia daily encreased, and he saw evidently how much he was beloved by that amiable girl: he was likewise strongly prepossessed with an idea of Charlotte's perfidy. What wonder then if he gave himself up to the delightful sensation which pervaded his bosom; and finding no obstacle arise to oppose his happiness, he solicited and obtained the hand of Julia. A few days before his marriage he thus addressed Belcour:

"Though Charlotte, by her abandoned conduct, has thrown herself from my protection, I still hold myself bound to support her till relieved from her present condition, and also to provide for the child. I do not intend to see her again, but I will place a sum of money in your hands, which will amply supply her with every convenience; but should she require more, let her have it, and I will see it repaid. I wish I could prevail on the poor deluded girl to return to her friends: she was an only child, and I make no doubt but that they would joyfully receive her; it would shock me greatly to see her henceforth leading a life of infamy, as I should always accuse myself of being the primary cause of all her errors. If she should chuse to remain under your protection, be kind to her, Belcour, I conjure you. Let not satiety prompt you to treat her in such a manner, as may drive her to actions which necessity might urge her to, while her better reason disapproved them: she shall never want a friend while I live, but I never more desire to behold her; her presence would be always painful to me, and a glance from her eye would call the blush of conscious guilt into my cheek.

"I will write a letter to her, which you may deliver when I am gone, as I shall go to St. Eustatia the day after my union with Julia, who will accompany me."

Belcour promised to fulfil the request of his friend, though nothing was farther from his intentions, than the least design of delivering the letter, or making Charlotte acquainted with the provision Montraville had made for her; he was bent on the complete ruin of the unhappy girl, and supposed, by reducing her to an entire dependance on him, to bring her by degrees to consent to gratify his ungenerous passion.

The evening before the day appointed for the nuptials of Montraville and Julia, the former retired early to his apartment; and ruminating on the past scenes of his life, suffered the keenest remorse in the remembrance of Charlotte's seduction. "Poor girl," said he, "I will at least write and bid her adieu; I will too endeavour to awaken that love of virtue in her bosom which her unfortunate attachment to me has extinguished." He took up the pen and began to write, but words were denied him. How could he address the woman whom he had seduced, and whom, though he thought unworthy his tenderness, he was about to bid adieu for ever? How should he tell her that he was going to abjure her, to enter into the most indissoluble ties with another, and that he could not even own the infant which she bore as his child? Several letters were begun and destroyed: at length he completed the following:

TO CHARLOTTE.

"Though I have taken up my pen to address you, my poor injured girl, I feel I am inadequate to the task; yet, however painful the endeavour, I could not resolve upon leaving you for ever without one kind line to bid you adieu, to tell you how my heart bleeds at the remembrance of what you was, before you saw the hated Montraville. Even now imagination paints the scene, when, torn by contending passions, when, struggling between love and duty, you fainted in my arms, and I lifted you into the chaise: I see the agony of your mind, when, recovering, you found yourself on the road to Portsmouth: but how, my gentle girl, how could you, when so justly impressed with the value of virtue, how could you, when loving as I thought you loved me, yield to the solicitations of Belcour?

"Oh Charlotte, conscience tells me it was I, villain that I am, who first taught you the allurements of guilty pleasure; it was I who dragged you from the calm repose which innocence and virtue ever enjoy; and can I, dare I tell you, it was not love prompted to the horrid deed? No, thou dear, fallen angel, believe your repentant Montraville, when he tells you the man who truly loves will never betray the object of his affection. Adieu, Charlotte: could you still find charms in a life of unoffending innocence, return to your parents; you shall never want the means of support both for yourself and child. Oh! gracious heaven! may that child be entirely free from the vices of its father and the weakness of its mother.

"To-morrow — but no, I cannot tell you what to-morrow will produce; Belcour will inform you: he also has cash for you, which I beg you will ask for whenever you may want it. Once more adieu: believe me could I hear you was returned to your friends, and enjoying that tranquillity of which I have robbed you, I should be as completely happy as even you, in your fondest hours, could wish me, but till then a gloom will obscure the brightest prospects of   MONTRAVILLE."

After he had sealed this letter he threw himself on the bed, and enjoyed a few hours repose. Early in the morning Belcour tapped at his door: he arose hastily, and prepared to meet his Julia at the altar.

"This is the letter to Charlotte," said he, giving it to Belcour: "take it to her when we are gone to Eustatia; and I conjure you, my dear friend, not to use any sophistical arguments to prevent her return to virtue; but should she incline that way, encourage her in the thought, and assist her to put her design in execution."

Chapter XXVII.

Pensive she mourn' d, and hung her languid head,
Like a fair lily overcharg'd with dew.

CHARLOTTE HAD NOW BEEN LEFT almost three months a prey to her own melancholy reflexions – sad companions indeed; nor did any one break in upon her solitude but Belcour, who once or twice called to enquire after her health, and tell her he had in vain endeavoured to bring Montraville to hear reason; and once, but only once, was her mind cheared by the receipt of an affectionate letter from Mrs. Beauchamp. Often had she wrote to her perfidious seducer, and with the most persuasive eloquence endeavoured to convince him of her innocence; but these letters were never suffered to reach the hands of Montraville, or they must, though on the very eve of marriage, have prevented his deserting the wretched girl. Real anguish of heart had in a great measure faded her charms, her cheeks were pale from want of rest, and her eyes, by frequent, indeed almost continued weeping, were sunk and heavy. Sometimes a gleam of hope would play about her heart when she thought of her parents – "They cannot surely," she would say, "refuse to forgive me; or should they deny their pardon to me, they will not hate my innocent infant on account of its mother's errors." How often did the poor mourner wish for the consoling presence of the benevolent Mrs. Beauchamp.

"If she were here," she would cry, "she would certainly comfort me, and sooth the distraction of my soul."

She was sitting one afternoon, wrapped in these melancholy reflexions, when she was interrupted by the entrance of Belcour. Great as the alteration was which incessant sorrow had made on her person, she was still interesting, still charming; and the unhallowed flame, which had urged Belcour to plant dissension between her and Montraville, still raged in his bosom: he was determined, if possible, to make her his mistress; nay, he had even conceived the diabolical scheme of taking her to New-York, and making her appear in every public place where it was likely she should meet Montraville, that he might be a witness to his unmanly triumph.

When he entered the room where Charlotte was sitting, he assumed the look of tender, consolatory friendship. "And how does my lovely Charlotte?" said he, taking her hand: "I fear you are not so well as I could wish."

"I am not well, Mr. Belcour," said she, "very far from it; but the pains and infirmities of the body I could easily bear, nay, submit to them with patience, were they not aggravated by the most insupportable anguish of my mind."

"You are not happy, Charlotte," said he, with a look of well-dissembled sorrow.

"Alas!" replied she mournfully, shaking her head, "how can I be happy, deserted and forsaken as I am, without a friend of my own sex to whom I can unburthen my full heart, nay, my fidelity suspected by the very man for whom I have sacrificed every thing valuable in life, for whom I have made myself a poor despised creature, an outcast from society, an object only of contempt and pity."

"You think too meanly of yourself, Miss Temple: there is no one who would dare to treat you with contempt: all who have the pleasure of knowing you must admire and esteem. You are lonely here, my dear girl; give me leave to conduct you to New-York, where the agreeable society of some ladies, to whom I will introduce you, will dispel these sad thoughts, and I shall again see returning chearfulness animate those lovely features."

"Oh never! never!" cried Charlotte, emphatically: "the virtuous part of my sex will scorn me, and I will never associate with infamy. No, Belcour, here let me hide my shame and sorrow, here let me spend my few remaining days in obscurity, unknown and unpitied, here let me die unlamented, and my name sink to oblivion." Here her tears stopped her utterance. Belcour was awed to silence: he dared not interrupt her; and after a moment's pause she proceeded — "I once had conceived the thought of going to New-York to seek out the still dear, though cruel, ungenerous Montraville, to throw myself at his feet, and entreat his compassion; heaven knows, not for myself; if I am no longer beloved, I will not be indebted to his pity to redress my injuries, but I would have knelt and entreated him not to forsake my poor unborn – " She could say no more; a crimson glow rushed over her cheeks, and covering her face with her hands, she sobbed aloud.

Something like humanity was awakened in Belcour's breast by this pathetic speech: he arose and walked towards the window; but the selfish passion which had taken possession of his heart, soon stifled these finer emotions; and he thought if Charlotte was once convinced she had no longer any dependance on Montraville, she would more readily throw herself on his protection. Determined, therefore, to inform her of all that had happened, he again resumed his seat; and finding she began to be more composed, enquired if she had ever heard from Montraville since the unfortunate recontre in her bed chamber.

"Ah no," said she. "I fear I shall never hear from him again."

"I am greatly of your opinion," said Belcour, "for he has been for some time past greatly attached—"

At the word "attached" a death-like paleness overspread the countenance of Charlotte, but she applied to some hartshorn[9] which stood beside her, and Belcour proceeded.

"He has been for some time past greatly attached to one Miss Franklin, a pleasing lively girl, with a large fortune."

"She may be richer, may be handsomer," cried Charlotte, "but cannot love him so well. Oh may she beware of his art, and not trust him too far as I have done."

"He addresses her publicly," said he, "and it was rumoured they were to be married before he sailed for Eustatia, whither his company is ordered."

"Belcour," said Charlotte, seizing his hand, and gazing at him earnestly, while her pale lips trembled with convulsive agony, "tell me, and tell me truly, I beseech you, do you think he can be such a villain as to marry another woman, and leave me to die with want and misery in a strange land: tell me what you think; I can bear it very well; I will not shrink from this heaviest stroke of fate; I have deserved my afflictions, and I will endeavour to bear them as I ought."

"I fear," said Belcour, "he can be that villain."

"Perhaps," cried she, eagerly interrupting him, "perhaps he is married already: come, let me know the worst," continued she with an affected look of composure: "you need not be afraid, I shall not send the fortunate lady a bowl of poison."

"Well then, my dear girl," said he, deceived by her appearance, "they were married on Thursday, and yesterday morning they sailed for Eustatia."

"Married—gone—say you?" cried she in a distracted accent, "what without a last farewell, without one thought on my unhappy situation! Oh Montraville, may God forgive your perfidy." She shrieked, and Belcour sprang forward just in time to prevent her falling to the floor.

---

9. *salt of hartshorn*: Made from the antlers of male red deer, and used as a smelling salt.

Alarming faintings now succeeded each other, and she was conveyed to her bed, from whence she earnestly prayed she might never more arise. Belcour staid with her that night, and in the morning found her in a high fever. The fits she had been seized with had greatly terrified him; and confined as she now was to a bed of sickness, she was no longer an object of desire: it is true for several days he went constantly to see her, but her pale, emaciated appearance disgusted him: his visits became less frequent; he forgot the solemn charge given him by Montraville; he even forgot the money entrusted to his care; and, the burning blush of indignation and shame tinges my cheek while I write it, this disgrace to humanity and manhood at length forgot even the injured Charlotte; and, attracted by the blooming health of a farmer's daughter, whom he had seen in his frequent excursions to the country, he left the unhappy girl to sink unnoticed to the grave, a prey to sickness, grief, and penury; while he, having triumphed over the virtue of the artless cottager, rioted in all the intemperance of luxury and lawless pleasure.

Chapter XXVIII.

A Trifling Retrospect

"BLESS MY HEART," cries my young, volatile reader, "I shall never have patience to get through these volumes, there are so many ahs! and ohs! so much fainting, tears, and distress, I am sick to death of the subject." My dear, chearful, innocent girl, for innocent I will suppose you to be, or you would acutely feel the woes of Charlotte, did conscience say, thus might it have been with me, had not Providence interposed to snatch me from destruction: therefore, my lively, innocent girl, I must request your patience: I am writing a tale of truth: I mean to write it to the heart: but if perchance the heart is rendered impenetrable by unbounded prosperity, or a continuance in vice, I expect not my tale to please, nay, I even expect it will be thrown by with disgust. But softly, gentle fair one; I pray you throw it not aside till you have perused the whole; mayhap you may find something therein to repay you for the trouble. Methinks I see a sarcastic smile sit on your countenance. – "And what," cry you, "does the conceited author suppose we can glean from these pages, if Charlotte is held up as an object of terror, to prevent us from falling into guilty errors? does not La Rue triumph in her shame, and by adding art to guilt, obtain the affection of a worthy man, and rise to a station where she is beheld with respect, and chearfully received into all companies. What then is the moral you would inculcate? Would you wish us to think that a deviation from virtue, if covered by art and hypocrisy, is not an object of detestation, but on the contrary shall raise us to fame and honour? while the hapless girl who falls a victim to her too great sensibility, shall be loaded with ignominy and shame?" No, my fair querist, I mean no such thing. Remember the endeavours of the wicked are often suffered to prosper, that in the end their fall may be attended with more bitterness of heart; while the cup of affliction is poured out for wise and salutary ends, and they who are compelled to drain it even to the bitter dregs, often find comfort at the bottom; the tear of penitence blots their offences from the book of fate, and they rise from the heavy, painful trial, purified and fit for a mansion in the kingdom of eternity.

Yes, my young friends, the tear of compassion shall fall for the fate of Charlotte, while the name of La Rue shall be detested and despised. For Charlotte, the soul melts with sympathy; for La Rue, it feels nothing but horror and contempt. But perhaps your gay hearts would rather follow the fortunate Mrs. Crayton through the scenes of pleasure and dissipation in which she was engaged, than listen to the complaints and miseries of Charlotte. I will for once oblige you; I will for once follow her to midnight revels, balls, and scenes of gaiety, for in such was she constantly engaged.

I have said her person was lovely; let us add that she was surrounded by splendor and affluence, and he must know but little of the world who can wonder, (however faulty such a woman's conduct,) at her being followed by the men, and her company courted by the women: in short Mrs. Crayton was the universal favourite: she set the fashions, she was toasted by all the gentlemen, and copied by all the ladies.

Colonel Crayton was a domestic man. Could he be happy with such a woman? impossible! Remonstrance was vain: he might as well have preached to the winds, as endeavour to persuade her from any action, however ridiculous, on which she had set her mind: in short, after a little ineffectual struggle, he gave up the attempt, and left her to follow the bent of her own inclinations: what those were, I think the reader must have seen enough of her character to form a just idea. Among the number who paid their devotions at her shrine, she singled one, a young Ensign of mean birth, indifferent education, and weak intellects. How such a man came into the army, we hardly know to account for, and how he afterwards rose to posts of honour is likewise strange and wonderful. But fortune is blind, and so are those too frequently who have the power of dispensing her favours: else why do we see fools and knaves at the very top of the wheel, while patient merit sinks to the extreme of the opposite abyss. But we may form a thousand conjectures on this subject, and yet never hit on the right. Let us therefore endeavour to deserve her smiles, and whether we succeed or not, we shall feel more innate satisfaction, than thousands of those who bask in the sunshine of her favour unworthily. But to return to Mrs. Crayton: this young man, whom I shall distinguish by the name of Corydon, was the reigning favourite of her heart. He escorted her to the play, danced with her at every ball, and when indisposition prevented her going out, it was he alone who was permitted to chear the gloomy solitude to which she was obliged to confine herself. Did she ever think of poor Charlotte? – if she did, my dear Miss, it was only to laugh at the poor girl's want of spirit in consenting to be moped up in the country, while Montraville was enjoying all the pleasures of a gay, dissipated city. When she heard of his marriage, she smiling said, so there's an end of Madam Charlotte's hopes. I wonder who will take her now, or what will become of the little affected prude?

But as you have lead to the subject, I think we may as well return to the distressed Charlotte, and not, like the unfeeling Mrs. Crayton, shut our hearts to the call of humanity.

Chapter XXIX.

We Go Forward Again

THE STRENGTH OF CHARLOTTE'S constitution combatted against her disorder, and she began slowly to recover, though she still laboured under a violent depression of spirits: how must that depression be encreased, when, upon examining her little store, she found herself reduced to one solitary guinea, and that during her illness the attendance of an apothecary and nurse, together with many other unavoidable expences, had involved her in debt, from which she saw no method of extricating herself. As to the faint hope which she had entertained of hearing from and being relieved by her parents; it now entirely forsook her, for it was above four months since her letter was dispatched, and she had received no answer: she therefore imagined that her conduct had either entirely alienated their affection from her, or broken their hearts, and she must never more hope to receive their blessing.

Never did any human being wish for death with greater fervency or with juster cause; yet she had too just a sense of the duties of the Christian religion to attempt to put a period to her own existence. "I have but to be patient a little longer," she would cry, "and nature, fatigued and fainting, will throw off this heavy load of mortality, and I shall be released from all my sufferings."

It was one cold stormy day in the latter end of December, as Charlotte sat by a handful of fire, the low state of her finances not allowing her to replenish her stock of fuel, and prudence teaching her to be careful of what she had, when she was surprised by the entrance of a farmer's wife, who, without much ceremony, seated herself, and began this curious harangue.

"I'm come to see if as how you can pay your rent, because as how we hear Captain Montable is gone away, and it's fifty to one if he b'ant killed afore he comes back again; an then, Miss, or Ma'am, or whatever you may be, as I was saying to my husband, where are we to look for our money."

This was a stroke altogether unexpected by Charlotte: she knew so little of the ways of the world that she had never bestowed a thought on the payment for the rent of the house; she knew indeed that she owed a good deal, but this was never reckoned among the others: she was thunderstruck; she hardly knew what answer to make, yet it was absolutely necessary that she should say something; and judging of the gentleness of every female disposition by her own, she thought the best way to interest the woman in her favour would be to tell her candidly to what a situation she was reduced, and how little probability there was of her ever paying any body.

Alas poor Charlotte, how confined was her knowledge of human nature, or she would have been convinced that the only way to insure the friendship and assistance of your surrounding acquaintance is to convince them you do not require it, for when once the petrifying aspect of distress and penury appear, whose qualities, like Medusa's head, can change to stone all that look upon it; when once this Gorgon claims acquaintance with us, the phantom of friendship, that before courted our notice, will vanish into unsubstantial air, and the whole world before us appear a barren waste. Pardon me, ye dear spirits of benevolence, whose benign smiles and chearful-giving hand have strewed sweet flowers on many a thorny path through which my wayward fate forced me to pass; think not, that, in condemning the unfeeling texture of the human heart, I forget the spring from whence flow all the comforts I enjoy: oh no! I look up to you as to bright constellations, gathering new splendours from the surrounding darkness; but ah! whilst I adore the benignant rays that cheared and illumined my heart, I mourn that their influence cannot extend to all the sons and daughters of affliction.

"Indeed, Madam," said poor Charlotte in a tremulous accent, "I am at a loss what to do. Montraville placed me here, and promised to defray all my expenses: but he has forgot his promise, he has forsaken me, and I have no friend who has either power or will to relieve me. Let me hope, as you see my unhappy situation, your charity – "

"Charity," cried the woman impatiently interrupting her, "charity indeed: why, Mistress, charity begins at home, and I have seven children at home, *honest, lawful* children, and it is my duty to keep them; and do you think I will give away my property to a nasty, impudent hussey, to maintain her and her bastard; an I was saying to my husband the other day what will this world come to; honest women are nothing now-a-days, while the harlotings are set up for fine ladies, and look upon us no more nor the dirt they walk upon: but let me tell you, my fine spoken Ma'am, I must have my money; so seeing as how you can't pay it, why you must troop, and leave all your fine gimcracks and fal der ralls behind you. I don't ask for no more nor my right, and nobody shall dare for to go for to hinder me of it."

"Oh heavens," cried Charlotte, clasping her hands, "what will become of me?"

"Come on ye!" retorted the unfeeling wretch: "why go to the barracks and work for a morsel of bread; wash and mend the soldier's cloaths, an cook their victuals, and not expect to live in idleness on honest people's means. Oh I wish I could see the day when all such cattle were obliged to work hard and eat little; it's only what they deserve."

"Father of mercy," cried Charlotte, "I acknowledge thy correction just; but prepare me, I beseech thee, for the portion of misery thou may'st please to lay upon me."

"Well," said the woman, "I shall go an tell my husband as how you can't pay; and so d'ye see, Ma'am, get ready to be packing away this very night, for you should not stay another night in this house, though I was sure you would lay in the street."

Charlotte bowed her head in silence; but the anguish of her heart was too great to permit her to articulate a single word.

Chapter XXX.

And what is friendship but a name,
   A charm that lulls to sleep,
A shade that follows wealth and fame,
   But leaves the wretch to weep.

WHEN CHARLOTTE WAS LEFT to herself, she began to think what course she must take, or to whom she could apply, to prevent her perishing for want, or perhaps that very night falling a victim to the inclemency of the season. After many perplexed thoughts, she at last determined to set out for New-York, and enquire out Mrs. Crayton, from whom she had no doubt but she should obtain immediate relief as soon as her distress was made known; she had no sooner formed this resolution than she resolved immediately to put it in execution: she therefore wrote the following little billet to Mrs. Crayton, thinking if she should have company with her it would be better to send it in than to request to see her.

To MRS. CRAYTON.

"MADAM,

"When we left our native land, that dear, happy land which now contains all that is dear to the wretched Charlotte, our prospects were the same; we both, pardon me, Madam, if I say, we both too easily followed the impulse of our treacherous hearts, and trusted our happiness on a tempestuous ocean, where mine has been wrecked and lost for ever; you have been more fortunate — you are united to a man of honour and humanity, united by the most sacred ties, respected, esteemed, and admired, and surrounded by innumerable blessings of which I am bereaved, enjoying those pleasures which have fled my bosom never to return; alas! sorrow and deep regret have taken their place. Behold me, Madam, a poor forsaken wanderer, who has no where to lay her weary head, wherewith to supply the wants of nature, or to shield her from the inclemency of the weather. To you I sue, to you I look for pity and relief. I ask not to be received as an intimate or an equal; only for charity's sweet sake receive me into your hospitable mansion, allot me the meanest apartment in it, and let me breath out my soul in prayers for your happiness; I cannot, I feel I cannot long bear up under the accumulated woes that pour in upon me; but oh! my dear Madam, for the love of heaven suffer me not to expire in the street; and when I am at peace, as soon I shall be, extend your compassion to my helpless offspring, should it please heaven that it should survive its unhappy mother. A gleam of joy breaks in on my benighted soul while I reflect that you cannot, will not refuse your protection to the heart-broken.   CHARLOTTE."

When Charlotte had finished this letter, late as it was in the afternoon, and though the snow began to fall very fast, she tied up a few necessaries which she had prepared against her expected confinement, and terrified lest she should be again exposed to the insults of her barbarous landlady, more dreadful to her wounded spirit than either storm or darkness, she set forward for New-York.

It may be asked by those, who, in a work of this kind, love to cavil at every trifling omission, whether Charlotte did not possess any valuable of which she could have disposed, and by that means have supported herself till Mrs. Beauchamp's return, when she would have been certain of receiving every tender attention which compassion and friendship could dictate: but let me entreat these wise, penetrating gentlemen to reflect, that when Charlotte left England, it was in such haste that there was no time to purchase any thing more than what was wanted for immediate use on the voyage, and after her arrival at New-York, Montraville's affection soon began to decline, so that her whole wardrobe consisted of only necessaries, and as to baubles, with which fond lovers often load their mistresses, she possessed not one, except a plain gold locket of small value, which contained a lock of her mother's hair, and which the greatest extremity of want could not have forced her to part with.

I hope, Sir, your prejudices are now removed in regard to the probability of my story? Oh they are. Well then, with your leave, I will proceed.

The distance from the house which our suffering heroine occupied, to New-York, was not very great, yet the snow fell so fast, and the cold so intense, that, being unable from her situation to walk quick, she found herself almost sinking with cold and fatigue before she reached the town; her garments, which were merely suitable to the summer season, being an undress robe of plain white muslin, were wet through, and a thin black cloak and bonnet, very improper habiliments for such a climate, but poorly defended her from the cold. In this situation she reached the city, and enquired of a foot soldier whom she met, the way to Colonel Crayton's.

"Bless you, my sweet lady," said the soldier with a voice and look of compassion, "I will shew you the way with all my heart; but if you are going to make a petition to Madam Crayton it is all to no purpose I assure you: if you please I will conduct you to Mr. Franklin's; though Miss Julia is married and gone now, yet the old gentleman is very good."

"Julia Franklin," said Charlotte; "is she not married to Montraville?"

"Yes," replied the soldier, "and may God bless them, for a better officer never lived, he is so good to us all; and as to Miss Julia, all the poor folk almost worshipped her."

"Gracious heaven," cried Charlotte, "is Montraville unjust then to none but me."

The soldier now shewed her Colonel Crayton's door, and, with a beating heart, she knocked for admission.

Chapter XXXI.

Subject Continued

WHEN THE DOOR WAS OPENED, Charlotte, in a voice rendered scarcely articulate, through cold and the extreme agitation of her mind, demanded whether Mrs. Crayton was at home. The servant hesitated: he knew that his lady was engaged at a game of picquet with her dear Corydon, nor could he think she would like to be disturbed by a person whose appearance spoke her of so little consequence as Charlotte; yet there was something in her countenance that rather interested him in her favour, and he said his lady was engaged, but if she had any particular message he would deliver it.

"Take up this letter," said Charlotte: "tell her the unhappy writer of it waits in her hall for an answer."

The tremulous accent, the tearful eye, must have moved any heart not composed of adamant. The man took the letter from the poor suppliant, and hastily ascended the stair case.

"A letter, Madam," said he, presenting it to his lady: "an immediate answer is required."

Mrs. Crayton glanced her eye carelessly over the contents. "What stuff is this;" cried she haughtily; "have not I told you a thousand times that I will not be plagued with beggars, and petitions from people one knows nothing about? Go tell the woman I can't do any thing in it. I'm sorry, but one can't relieve every body."

The servant bowed, and heavily returned with this chilling message to Charlotte.

"Surely," said she, "Mrs. Crayton has not read my letter. Go, my good friend, pray go back to her; tell her it is Charlotte Temple who requests beneath her hospitable roof to find shelter from the inclemency of the season."

"Prithee, don't plague me, man," cried Mrs. Crayton impatiently, as the servant advanced something in behalf of the unhappy girl. "I tell you I don't know her."

"Not know me," cried Charlotte, rushing into the room, (for she had followed the man up stairs) "not know me, not remember the ruined Charlotte Temple, who, but for you, perhaps might still have been innocent, still have been happy. Oh! La Rue, this is beyond every thing I could have believed possible."

"Upon my honour, Miss," replied the unfeeling woman with the utmost effrontery, "this is a most unaccountable address: it is beyond my comprehension. John," continued she, turning to the servant, "the young woman is certainly out of her senses: do pray take her away, she terrifies me to death."

"Oh God," cried Charlotte, clasping her hands in an agony, "this is too much; what will become of me? but I will not leave you; they shall not tear me from you; here on my knees I conjure you to save me from perishing in the streets; if you really have forgot me, oh for charity's sweet sake this night let me be sheltered from the winter's piercing cold."

The kneeling figure of Charlotte in her affecting situation might have moved the heart of a stoic to compassion; but Mrs. Crayton remained inflexible. In vain did Charlotte recount the time they had known each other at Chichester, in vain mention their being in the same ship, in vain were the names of Montraville and Belcour mentioned. Mrs. Crayton could only say she was sorry for her imprudence, but could not think of having her own reputation endangered by encouraging a woman of that kind in her own house, besides she did not know what trouble and expense she might bring upon her husband by giving shelter to a woman in her situation.

"I can at least die here," said Charlotte, "I feel I cannot long survive this dreadful conflict. Father of mercy, here let me finish my existence." Her agonizing sensations overpowered her, and she fell senseless on the floor.

"Take her away," said Mrs. Crayton, "she will really frighten me into hysterics; take her away I say this instant."

"And where must I take the poor creature?" said the servant with a voice and look of compassion.

"Any where," cried she hastily, "only don't let me ever see her again. I declare she has flurried me so I shan't be myself again this fortnight."

John, assisted by his fellow-servant, raised and carried her down stairs. "Poor soul," said he, "you shall not lay in the street this night. I have a bed and a poor little hovel, where my wife and her little ones rest them, but they shall watch to night, and you shall be sheltered from danger." They placed her in a chair; and the benevolent man, assisted by one of his comrades, carried her to the place where his wife and children lived. A surgeon was sent for: he bled her, she gave signs of returning life, and before the dawn gave birth to a female infant. After this event she lay for some hours in a kind of stupor; and if at any time she spoke, it was with a quickness and incoherence that plainly evinced the total deprivation of her reason.

Chapter XXXII.

Reasons Why and Wherefore

THE READER OF SENSIBILITY may perhaps be astonished to find Mrs. Crayton could so positively deny any knowledge of Charlotte; it is therefore but just that her conduct should in some measure be accounted for. She had ever been fully sensible of the superiority of Charlotte's sense and virtue; she was conscious that she had never swerved from rectitude, had it not been for her bad precepts and worse example. These were things as yet unknown to her husband, and she wished not to have that part of her conduct exposed to him, as she had great reason to fear she had already lost considerable part of that power she once maintained over him. She trembled whilst Charlotte was in the house, lest the Colonel should return; she perfectly well remembered how much he seemed interested in her favour whilst on their passage from England, and made no doubt, but, should he see her in her present distress, he would offer her an asylum, and protect her to the utmost of his power. In that case she feared the unguarded nature of Charlotte might discover to the Colonel the part she had taken in the unhappy girl's elopement, and she well knew the contrast between her own and Charlotte's conduct would make the former appear in no very respectable light. Had she reflected properly, she would have afforded the poor girl protection; and by enjoining her silence, ensured it by acts of repeated kindness; but vice in general blinds its votaries, and they discover their real characters to the world when they are most studious to preserve appearances.

Just so it happened with Mrs. Crayton: her servants made no scruple of mentioning the cruel conduct of their lady to a poor distressed lunatic who claimed her protection; every one joined in reprobating her inhumanity; nay even Corydon thought she might at least have ordered her to be taken care of, but he dare not even hint it to her, for he lived but in her smiles, and drew from her lavish fondness large sums to support an extravagance to which the state of his own finances was very inadequate; it cannot therefore be supposed that he wished Mrs. Crayton to be very liberal in her bounty to the afflicted suppliant; yet vice had not so entirely seared over his heart, but the sorrows of Charlotte could find a vulnerable part.

Charlotte had now been three days with her humane preservers, but she was totally insensible of every thing: she raved incessantly for Montraville and her father: she was not conscious of being a mother, nor took the least notice of her child except to ask whose it was, and why it was not carried to its parents.

"Oh," said she one day, starting up on hearing the infant cry, "why, why will you keep that child here; I am sure you would not if you knew how hard it was for a mother to be parted from her infant: it is like tearing the cords of life asunder. Oh could you see the horrid sight which I now behold – there – there stands my dear mother, her poor bosom bleeding at every vein, her gentle, affectionate heart torn in a thousand pieces, and all for the loss of a ruined, ungrateful child. Save me – save me – from her frown. I dare not – indeed I dare not speak to her."

Such were the dreadful images that haunted her distracted mind, and nature was sinking fast under the dreadful malady which medicine had no power to remove. The surgeon who attended her was a humane man; he exerted his utmost abilities to save her, but he saw she was in want of many necessaries and comforts, which the poverty of her hospitable host rendered him unable to provide: he therefore determined to make her situation known to some of the officers' ladies, and endeavour to make a collection for her relief.

When he returned home, after making this resolution, he found a message from Mrs. Beauchamp, who had just arrived from Rhode-Island, requesting he would call and see one of her children, who was very unwell. "I do not know," said he, as he was hastening to obey the summons, "I do not know a woman to whom I could apply with more hope of success than Mrs. Beauchamp. I will endeavour to interest her in this poor girl's behalf; she wants the soothing balm of friendly consolation: we may perhaps save her; we will try at least."

"And where is she," cried Mrs. Beauchamp when he had prescribed something for the child, and told his little pathetic tale, "where is she, Sir?

we will go to her immediately. Heaven forbid that I should be deaf to the calls of humanity. Come we will go this instant." Then seizing the doctor's arm, they sought the habitation that contained the dying Charlotte.

Chapter XXXIII.

Which People Void of Feeling Need Not Read

WHEN MRS. BEAUCHAMP ENTERED the apartment of the poor sufferer, she started back with horror. On a wretched bed, without hangings and but poorly supplied with covering, lay the emaciated figure of what still retained the semblance of a lovely woman, though sickness had so altered her features that Mrs. Beauchamp had not the least recollection of her person. In one corner of the room stood a woman washing, and, shivering over a small fire, two healthy but half naked children; the infant was asleep beside its mother, and, on a chair by the bed side, stood a porrenger and wooden spoon, containing a little gruel, and a tea-cup with about two spoonfulls of wine in it. Mrs. Beauchamp had never before beheld such a scene of poverty; she shuddered involuntarily, and exclaiming – "heaven preserve us!" leaned on the back of a chair ready to sink to the earth. The doctor repented having so precipitately brought her into this affecting scene; but there was no time for apologies: Charlotte caught the sound of her voice, and starting almost out of bed, exclaimed – "Angel of peace and mercy, art thou come to deliver me? Oh, I know you are, for whenever you was near me I felt eased of half my sorrows; but you don't know me, nor can I, with all the recollection I am mistress of, remember your name just now, but I know that benevolent countenance, and the softness of that voice which has so often comforted the wretched Charlotte."

Mrs. Beauchamp had, during the time Charlotte was speaking, seated herself on the bed and taken one of her hands; she looked at her attentively, and at the name of Charlotte she perfectly conceived the whole shocking affair. A faint sickness came over her. "Gracious heaven," said she, "is this possible?" and bursting into tears, she reclined the burning head of Charlotte on her own bosom; and folding her arms about her, wept over her in silence. "Oh," said Charlotte, "you are very good to weep thus for me: it is a long time since I shed a tear for myself: my head and heart are both on fire, but these tears of your's seem to cool and refresh it. Oh now I remember you said you would send a letter to my poor father: do you think he ever received it? or perhaps you have brought me an answer: why don't you speak, Madam? Does he say I may go home? Well he is very good; I shall soon be ready."

She then made an effort to get out of bed; but being prevented, her frenzy again returned, and she raved with the greatest wildness and incoherence. Mrs. Beauchamp, finding it was impossible for her to be removed, contented herself with ordering the apartment to be made more comfortable, and procuring a proper nurse for both mother and child; and having learnt the particulars of Charlotte's fruitless application to Mrs. Crayton from honest John, she amply rewarded him for his benevolence, and returned home with a heart oppressed with many painful sensations, but yet rendered easy by the reflexion that she had performed her duty towards a distressed fellow-creature.

Early the next morning she again visited Charlotte, and found her tolerably composed; she called her by name, thanked her for her goodness, and when her child was brought to her, pressed it in her arms, wept over it, and called it the offspring of disobedience. Mrs. Beauchamp was delighted to see her so much amended, and began to hope she might recover, and, spite of her former errors, become an useful and respectable member of society; but the arrival of the doctor put an end to these delusive hopes: he said nature was making her last effort, and a few hours would most probably consign the unhappy girl to her kindred dust.

Being asked how she found herself, she replied – "Why better, much better, doctor. I hope now I have but little more to suffer. I had last night a few hours sleep, and when I awoke recovered the full power of recollection. I am quite sensible of my weakness; I feel I have but little longer to combat with the shafts of affliction. I have an humble confidence in the mercy of him who died to save the world, and trust that my sufferings in this state of mortality, joined to my unfeigned repentance, through his mercy, have blotted my offences from the sight of my offended maker. I have but one care – my poor infant! Father of mercy," continued she, raising her eyes, "of thy infinite goodness, grant that the sins of the parent be not visited on the unoffending child. May those who taught me to despise thy laws be forgiven; lay not my offences to their charge, I beseech thee; and oh! shower the choicest of thy blessings on those whose pity has soothed the afflicted heart, and made easy even the bed of pain and sickness."

She was exhausted by this fervent address to the throne of mercy, and though her lips still moved her voice became inarticulate: she lay for some time as it were in a doze, and then recovering, faintly pressed Mrs. Beauchamp's hand, and requested that a clergyman might be sent for.

On his arrival she joined fervently in the pious office, frequently mentioning her ingratitude to her parents as what lay most heavy at her heart. When she had performed the last solemn duty, and was preparing to lie down, a little bustle on the outside door occasioned Mrs. Beauchamp to open it, and enquire the cause. A man in appearance about forty, presented himself, and asked for Mrs. Beauchamp.

"That is my name, Sir," said she.

"Oh then, my dear Madam," cried he, "tell me where I may find my poor, ruined, but repentant child."

Mrs. Beauchamp was surprised and affected; she knew not what to say; she foresaw the agony this interview would occasion Mr. Temple, who had just arrived in search of his Charlotte, and yet was sensible that the pardon and blessing of her father would soften even the agonies of death to the daughter.

She hesitated. "Tell me, Madam," cried he wildly, "tell me, I beseech thee, does she live? shall I see my darling once again? Perhaps she is in this house. Lead, lead me to her, that I may bless her, and then lie down and die."

The ardent manner in which he uttered these words occasioned him to raise his voice. It caught the ear of Charlotte: she knew the beloved sound: and uttering a loud shriek, she sprang forward as Mr. Temple entered the room. "My adored father." "My long lost child." Nature could support no more, and they both sunk lifeless into the arms of the attendants.

Charlotte was again put into bed, and a few moments restored Mr. Temple: but to describe the agony of his sufferings is past the power of any one, who, though they may readily conceive, cannot delineate the dreadful scene. Every eye gave testimony of what each heart felt – but all were silent.

When Charlotte recovered, she found herself supported in her father's arms. She cast on him a most expressive look, but was unable to speak. A reviving cordial was administered. She then asked, in a low voice, for her child: it was brought to her: she put it in her father's arms. "Protect her," said she, "and bless your dying –"

Unable to finish the sentence, she sunk back on her pillow: her countenance was serenely composed; she regarded her father as he pressed the infant to his breast with a steadfast look; a sudden beam of joy passed across her languid features, she raised her eyes to heaven – and then closed them for ever.

Chapter XXXIV.

Retribution

IN THE MEAN TIME Montraville having received orders to return to New-York, arrived, and having still some remains of compassionate tenderness for the woman whom he regarded as brought to shame by himself, he went out in search of Belcour, to enquire whether she was safe, and whether the child lived. He found him immersed in dissipation, and could gain no other intelligence than that Charlotte had left him, and that he knew not what was become of her.

"I cannot believe it possible," said Montraville, "that a mind once so pure as Charlotte Temple's, should so suddenly become the mansion of vice. Beware, Belcour," continued he, "beware if you have dared to behave either unjust or dishonourably to that poor girl, your life shall pay the forfeit: – I will revenge her cause."

He immediately went into the country, to the house where he had left Charlotte. It was desolate. After much enquiry he at length found the servant girl who had lived with her. From her he learnt the misery Charlotte had endured from the complicated evils of illness, poverty, and a broken heart, and that she had set out on foot for New-York, on a cold winter's evening; but she could inform him no further.

Tortured almost to madness by this shocking account, he returned to the city, but, before he reached it, the evening was drawing to a close. In entering the town he was obliged to pass several little huts, the residence of poor women who supported themselves by washing the cloaths of the officers and soldiers. It was nearly dark: he heard from a neighbouring steeple a solemn toll that seemed to say some poor mortal was going to their last mansion: the sound struck on the heart of Montraville, and he involuntarily stopped, when, from one of the houses, he saw the appearance of a funeral. Almost unknowing what he did, he followed at a small distance; and as they let the coffin into the grave, he enquired of a soldier who stood by, and had just brushed off a tear that did honour to his heart, who it was that was just buried. "An please your honour," said the man, "'tis a poor girl that was brought from her friends by a cruel man, who left her when she was big with child, and married another." Montraville stood motionless, and the man proceeded – "I met her myself not a fortnight since one night all wet and cold in the streets; she went to Madam Crayton's, but she would not take her in, and so the poor thing went raving mad." Montraville could bear no more; he struck his hands against his forehead with violence; and exclaiming "poor murdered Charlotte!" ran with precipitation towards the place where they were heaping the earth on her remains. "Hold, hold, one moment," said he. "Close not the grave of the injured Charlotte Temple till I have taken vengeance on her murderer."

"Rash young man," said Mr. Temple, "who art thou that thus disturbest the last mournful rites of the dead, and rudely breakest in upon the grief of an afflicted father."

"If thou art the father of Charlotte Temple," said he, gazing at him with mingled horror and amazement – "if thou art her father – I am Montraville." Then falling on his knees, he continued – "Here is my bosom. I bare it to receive the stroke I merit. Strike – strike now, and save me from the misery of reflection."

"Alas!" said Mr. Temple, "if thou wert the seducer of my child, thy own reflexions be thy punishment. I wrest not the power from the hand of omnipotence. Look on that little heap of earth, there hast thou buried the only joy of a fond father. Look at it often; and may thy heart feel such true sorrow as shall merit the mercy of heaven." He turned from him; and Montraville starting up from the ground, where he had thrown himself, and at that instant remembering the perfidy of Belcour, flew like lightning to his lodgings. Belcour was intoxicated; Montraville impetuous: they fought, and the sword of the latter entered the heart of his adversary. He fell, and expired almost instantly. Montraville had received a slight wound; and overcome with the agitation of his mind and loss of blood, was carried in a state of insensibility to his distracted wife. A dangerous illness and obstinate delirium ensued, during which he raved incessantly for Charlotte: but a strong constitution, and the tender assiduities of Julia, in time overcame the disorder. He recovered; but to the end of his life was subject to severe fits of melancholy, and while he remained at New-York frequently retired to the church-yard, where he would weep over the grave, and regret the untimely fate of the lovely Charlotte Temple.

Chapter XXXV.

Conclusion

SHORTLY AFTER THE INTERMENT of his daughter, Mr. Temple, with his dear little charge and her nurse, set forward for England. It would be impossible to do justice to the meeting scene between him, his Lucy, and her aged father. Every heart of sensibility can easily conceive their feelings. After the first tumult of grief was subsided, Mrs. Temple gave up the chief of her time to her grand-child, and as she grew up and improved, began to almost fancy she again possessed her Charlotte.

It was about ten years after these painful events, that Mr. and Mrs. Temple, having buried their father, were obliged to come to London on particular business, and brought the little Lucy with them. They had been walking one evening, when on their return they found a poor wretch sitting on the steps of the door. She attempted to rise as they approached, but from extreme weakness was unable, and after several fruitless efforts fell back in a fit. Mr. Temple was not one of those men who stand to consider whether by assisting an object in distress they shall not inconvenience themselves, but instigated by the impulse of a noble feeling heart, immediately ordered her to be carried into the house, and proper restoratives applied.

She soon recovered; and fixing her eyes on Mrs. Temple, cried – "You know not, Madam, what you do; you know not whom you are relieving, or you would curse me in the bitterness of your heart. Come not near me, Madam, I shall contaminate you. I am the viper that stung your peace. I am the woman who turned the poor Charlotte out to perish in the street. Heaven have mercy! I see her now," continued she looking at Lucy; "such, such was the fair bud of innocence that my vile arts blasted ere it was half blown."

It was in vain that Mr. and Mrs. Temple intreated her to be composed and to take some refreshment. She only drank half a glass of wine; and then told them that she had been separated from her husband seven years, the chief of which she had passed in riot, dissipation, and vice, till, overtaken by poverty and sickness, she had been reduced to part with every valuable, and thought only of ending her life in a prison; when a benevolent friend paid her debts and released her; but that her illness encreasing, she had no possible means of supporting herself, and her friends were weary of relieving her. "I have fasted," said she, "two days, and last night lay my aching head on the cold pavement: indeed it was but just that I should experience those miseries myself which I had unfeelingly inflicted on others."

Greatly as Mr. Temple had reason to detest Mrs. Crayton, he could not behold her in this distress without some emotions of pity. He gave her shelter that night beneath his hospitable roof, and the next day got her admission into an hospital; where having lingered a few weeks, she died, a striking example that vice, however prosperous in the beginning, in the end leads only to misery and shame.

FINIS.

Suggestions for Further Reading and Research

CONTEXTS

Bloch, Ruth H. "Changing Conceptions of Sexuality and Romance in Eighteenth-Century America." *William and Mary Quarterly*, third series, 60.1 (January 2003): 13-42. In a special issue of the journal devoted to "Sexuality in Early America," Bloch examines eighteenth-century attitudes toward sex (as opposed to sexual practice) and emerging ideas of romantic love. She includes the sentimental novel among her major source materials.

Bloch, Ruth H. *Gender and Morality in Anglo-American Culture, 1650–1800*. Berkeley: University of California Press, 2003. A collection of essays on North American women's history written between 1978 and 2001. Three of the essays provide particularly relevant contexts for *Charlotte Temple*: "Religion, Literary Sentimentalism, and Popular Revolutionary Ideology"; "The Gendered Meanings of Virtue in Revolutionary America"; and "Gender and the Public/Private Dichotomy in American Revolutionary Thought."

Burstein, Andrew. *Sentimental Democracy: The Evolution of America's Romantic Self-Image.* New York: Hill & Wang, 1999. Probes the affective or emotional sources of America's self-image in the period from 1750 to 1828. Burstein argues that the sentimental sources of American patriotism used myths of human potential in a "new land" to define national identity.

Coultrap-McQuin, Susan. *Doing Literary Business: American Women Writers in the Nineteenth Century.* Chapel Hill: University of North Carolina Press, 1990. Explores American women writers in the marketplace. While Coultrap-McQuin focuses primarily on a later time period than that of Rowson's career, her arguments reinforce an understanding that authorship was a profession for women as well as for men, and that literary economics could be brutal.

Davidson, Cathy N. *Revolution and the Word: The Rise of the Novel in America.* Expanded edition. 1986; New York: Oxford University Press, 2004. Groundbreaking history of the early American novel in three categories—novels of seduction, picaresque wandering, and gothic horror—which tracks how a community of readers used fiction as a tool for debating and shaping national identity.

Fliegelman, Jay. *Prodigals and Pilgrims: The American Revolution against Patriarchal Authority, 1750-1800.* Cambridge: Cambridge University Press, 1982. A pivotal study of eighteenth-century changes in the ideology of the American family. Fliegelman uses interdisciplinary and multinational sources to make a case that patriarchal family authority was replaced by more affectionate and egalitarian relationships between parents and children. In a nation given to using patterns of family life as figures for national identity, this raised questions about the nature of authority itself.

Kelley, Mary. *Learning to Stand & Speak: Women, Education, and Public Life in America's Republic.* Chapel Hill: University of North Carolina Press, 2006. Explores the role of schooling, especially at female academies and seminaries, as significant for shaping a transformation of women's individual and social identities in the post-Revolutionary and antebellum United States.

Lewis, Jan. "The Republican Wife: Virtue and Seduction in the Early Republic." *William and Mary Quarterly,* third series, 64 (1987): 689-721. Draws on popular literary and didactic works to argue that changing metaphors of marriage and family life opened political as well as domestic discussions about authority in the new United States.

Tompkins, Jane P. *Sensational Designs: The Cultural Work of American Fiction, 1790-1860.* New York: Oxford University Press, 1985. Tompkins was among the earliest to resist nineteenth- and twentieth-century derogatory evaluations of the sentimental novel. In "Sentimental Power: *Uncle Tom's Cabin* and the Politics of Literary History," she explores the uses of sentimentality, arguing that it became a significant agent for social change.

Winans, Robert B. "The Growth of a Novel-Reading Public in Late-Eighteenth-Century America." *Early American Literature* 9 (1975): 267-75. Contests the misconception that readers in the new United States seldom read fiction.

Woodmansee, Martha. "The Genius and the Copyright: Economic and Legal Conditions of the Emergence of the 'Author.'" *Eighteenth-Century Studies* 17 (Summer 1984): 425-48. Traces the concept of authorship from a craft with prescribed rules and conventions to a visionary process whereby unique individuals create original works.

Zagarri, Rosemarie. "The Rights of Man and Woman in Post-Revolutionary America." *William and Mary Quarterly*, third series, 55 (April 1998): 203-30. Probes the intellectual traditions that became the basis for differentiating between the political rights of men and women in the early United States.

SELECTED STUDIES OF ROWSON AND HER WORK

Baym, Nina. *American Women Writers and the Work of History, 1790-1860.* New Brunswick, NJ: Rutgers University Press, 1995. Includes Rowson in this study of American women who wrote history and, in the process, wrote themselves into a public sphere conventionally reserved for men.

Brandt, Ellen B. *Susanna Haswell Rowson: America's First Best-Selling Novelist.* Chicago: Serbra Press, 1975. A critical biography.

Davidson, Cathy N. "The Life and Times of *Charlotte Temple*: The Biography of a Book." In *Reading in America: Literature and Social History.* Ed. Cathy N. Davidson. Baltimore: Johns Hopkins University Press, 1989. 157-79. A thorough and engaging account of *Charlotte Temple* from the perspective of the history of the book.

Forcey, Blythe. "*Charlotte Temple* and the End of Epistolarity." *American Literature* 63.2 (1991): 225-41. Explores the effect of Rowson's break from the epistolary tradition in *Charlotte Temple.*

Homestead, Melissa J. "The Beginnings of the American Novel." In *The Oxford Handbook of Early American Literature.* Ed. Kevin J. Hayes. New York: Oxford University Press, 2008. Traces the origins of the American novel as a transatlantic phenomenon, using three Rowson novels, including *Charlotte Temple*, as examples.

Parker, Patricia L. *Susanna Rowson.* Boston: Twayne, 1986. Contains the fullest biographical account to date.

Rust, Marion. *Prodigal Daughters: Susanna Rowson's Early American Women.* Chapel Hill: University of North Carolina Press, 2008. A thoroughly researched study of Rowson's career and writing, emphasizing her attention to female agency and activism in early American gender practice.

Smith-Rosenberg, Carroll. "Subject Female: Authorizing American Identity." *American Literary History* 5 (1993): 481-511. Uses Charles Brockden Brown's

Edgar Huntly and Susanna Rowson's *Charlotte Temple* to trace the ways in which British North Americans reinvented themselves as citizens of a new nation.

Stern, Julia A. "Working through the Frame: The Dream of Transparency in *Charlotte Temple*." In *The Plight of Feeling: Sympathy and Dissent in the Early American Novel*. Chicago: University of Chicago Press, 1997. 31–69. Presents a reading of *Charlotte Temple* that emphasizes the narrator as a symbolic mother central to the novel's cultural work.

Vail, R. W. G. "Susanna Haswell Rowson, the Author of *Charlotte Temple*: A Bibliographical Study." *Proceedings of the American Antiquarian Society* 42 (1932): 47–160. Describes and catalogs 160 of the more than 200 editions of *Charlotte Temple*.

Weil, Dorothy. *In Defense of Women: Susanna Rowson (1762–1824)*. University Park: Pennsylvania State University Press, 1976. A bio-critical study that emphasizes feminist intentions and outcomes in Rowson's writing.

MANUSCRIPT SOURCES

A substantial collection of the Papers of Susanna Rowson (MSS 7379) are available through the Clifton Waller Barrett Library of American Literature, Special Collections, University of Virginia Library.

WEB SITES

<http://people.virginia.edu/~sfr/enam854/ctemple.html>   Excerpts   four nineteenth- and early-twentieth-century reviews of *Charlotte Temple*.

<http://etext.virginia.edu/toc/modeng/public/RowChar.html> Features the Francis Whiting Halsey edition of *Charlotte Temple: A Tale of Truth* (1905), the first scholarly edition. Though dated, the front matter is still of interest, and Halsey includes several illustrations.

Glossary of Literary Terms

Abstract language Any language that employs intangible, nonspecific concepts. *Love, truth,* and *beauty* are abstractions. Abstract language is the opposite of concrete language. Both types have different effects and are important features of an author's style.

Allegory A narrative in which persons, objects, settings, or events represent general concepts, moral qualities, or other abstractions.

Antagonist A character in some fiction, whose motives and actions work against, or are thought to work against, those of the hero, or protagonist. The conflict between these characters shapes the plot of their story.

Archetype A term introduced in the 1930s by psychologist C. G. Jung, who described archetypes as "primordial images" repeated throughout human history. Archetypes, or archetypal patterns, recur in myths, religion, dreams, fantasies, and art, and are said to have power because we know them, even if unconsciously. In literature, archetypes appear in character types, plot patterns, and descriptions.

Characterization Characterization means the development of a character or characters throughout a story. Characterization includes the narrator's description of what characters look like and what they think, say, and do (these are sometimes very dissimilar). Their own actions and views of themselves, and other characters' views of and behavior toward them, are also means of characterization.

Characters One of the elements of fiction, characters are usually the people of a work of literature; characters may be animals or some other beings. Characters are those about whom a story is told and sometimes, too, the ones telling the story. Characters may be minor or major, depending on their importance to a story.

Climax The moment of greatest intensity and conflict in the action of a story is its climax.

Concrete language Any specific, physical language that appeals to one or more of the senses—sight, hearing, taste, smell, or touch. *Stones*, *chairs*, and *hands* are concrete words. Concrete language is the opposite of abstract language. Both types are important features of an author's style.

Conflict Antagonism between characters, ideas, or lines of action; between one character and the outside world; or between aspects of a character's own nature. Conflict is essential in a traditional plot.

Description Language that presents specific features of a character, object, or setting, or the details of an action or event.

Dialogue Words spoken by characters, often in the form of conversation between two or more. In stories and other forms of prose, dialogue is commonly enclosed between quotation marks. Dialogue is an important element in characterization and plot.

Diction A writer's selection of words. Particular patterns or arrangements of words in sentences and paragraphs constitute prose style. Hemingway's diction is said to be precise, concrete, and economical.

Didactic fiction A kind of fiction that is designed to present or demonstrate a moral, religious, political, or other belief or position. Didactic works are different from purely imaginative ones, which are written for their inherent interest and value. The distinction between imaginative and didactic writing is not always sharp.

Elements of fiction Major elements of fiction are plot, characters, setting, point of view, style, and theme. Skillful employment of these entities is essential in effective novels and stories. From beginning to end, each element is active and relates to the others dynamically.

Epiphany In literature, epiphany describes a sudden illumination of the significance or true meaning of a person, place, thing, idea, or situation. Often a word, gesture, or other action reveals the significance. The term was popularized by James Joyce, who explained it fully in his autobiographical novel *Stephen Hero* (written in 1914; pub. 1944).

Fiction Traditionally, a prose narrative whose plot, characters, and settings are constructions of its writer's imagination, which draws on his or her experiences and reflections. Short stories are comparatively short works of fiction, novels long ones.

Figurative language Suggestive, rather than literal, language employing metaphor, simile, or other figures of speech.

First-person narrator See **point of view.**

Flashback A writer's way of introducing important earlier material. As a narrator tells a story, he or she may stop the flow of events and direct the reader to an earlier time. Sometimes the reader is returned to the present, sometimes kept in the past.

Foreshadowing Words, gestures, and other actions that suggest future events or outcomes. An example would be a character's saying, "I've got a bad feeling about this," and later in the narration something "bad" does happen to the character.

Genre A type or form of literature. The major literary genres are fiction, drama, poetry, and exposition (essay or book-length biography, criticism, history, and so on). Subgenres of fiction are the novel and the short story.

Image A word or group of words evoking concrete visual, auditory, or tactile associations. An image, sometimes called a "word-picture," is an important instance of figurative language.

Interior monologue An extended speech or narrative, presumed to be thought rather than spoken by a character. Interior monologues are similar to, but different from, *stream of consciousness*, which describes mental life at the border of consciousness. Interior monologues are typically more consciously controlled and conventionally structured, however private their thoughts.

Irony A way of writing or speaking that asserts the opposite of what the author, reader, and character know to be true. *Verbal* or *rhetorical* irony accomplishes these contradictory meanings by direct misstatements. *Situational* irony is achieved when events in a narrative turn out to be very different from, or even opposite to, what is expected.

Narrative A narrator's story of characters and events over a period of time. Usually the characters can be analyzed and generally understood; usually the events proceed in a cause-and-effect relation; and usually some unity can be found among the characters, plot, point of view, style, and theme of a narrative. Novels as well as stories are usually narratives, and journalism commonly employs narrative form.

Narrator The storyteller, usually an observer who is narrating in the *third-person point of view*, or a participant in the story's action speaking in the first person. Style and tone are important clues to the nature of a narrator and the validity and objectivity of the story itself. Sometimes a narrator who takes part in the action is too emotionally involved to be trusted for objectivity or accuracy. This narrator would be called an *unreliable narrator*.

Naturalism A literary movement that began in France in the late nineteenth century, spread, moderated, and influenced much twentieth-century literature. The movement, which started in reaction against the antiscientific sentimentality of the period, borrowed from the principles, aims, and methods of scientific thinkers such as Darwin and Spencer. Early naturalists held that human lives are determined externally by society and internally by drives and instincts and that free will is an illusion. Writers were to proceed in a reporterlike, objective manner. Stephen Crane shows the influence of early naturalism, Ernest Hemingway of later, more moderate, naturalism.

Novel An extended prose narrative or work of prose fiction, usually published alone. Hawthorne's *The Scarlet Letter* is a fairly short novel, Melville's *Moby-Dick, or, the Whale* a very long one. The length of a novel enables its author to develop characters, plot, and settings in greater detail than a short story writer can.

Novella Between the short story and the novel in size and complexity. Like them, the novella is a work of prose fiction. Sometimes it is called a long short story.

Omniscient narrator See **point of view**.

Parable A simple story that illustrates a moral point or teaches a lesson. The persons, places, things, and events are connected by the moral question only. The moral position of a parable is developed through the choices of people who believe and act in certain ways and are not abstract personifications as in allegory, nor animal characters as in folktales.

Parody Usually, a comic or satirical imitation of a serious piece of writing, exaggerating its weaknesses and ignoring its strengths. Its distinctive features are ridiculed through exaggeration and inappropriate placement in the parody.

Plot One of the elements of fiction, plot is the sequence of major events in a story, usually in a cause-effect relation. Plot and character are intimately related, since characters carry out the plot's action. Plots may be described as simple or complex, depending on their degree of complication. "Traditional" writers usually plot their stories tightly; modernist writers employ looser, often ambiguous plots.

Point of view One of the elements of fiction, point of view is the perspective, or angle of vision, from which a narrator presents a story. Point of view tells us about the narrator as well as about the characters, setting, and theme of a story. Two common points of view are *first-person narration* and *third-person narration*. If a narrator speaks of himself or herself as "I," the narration is in the first person; if the narrator's self is not apparent and the story is told about others from some distance, using "he," "she," "it," and "they," then third-person narration is likely in force. The point of view may be *omniscient* (all-knowing) or *limited.* When determining a story's point of view, it is helpful to decide whether the narrator is reporting events as they are happening or as they happened in the past; is observing or participating in the action; and is or is not emotionally involved.

Protagonist   The hero or main character of a narrative or drama. The action is the presentation and resolution of the protagonist's conflict, internal or external; if the conflict is with another major character, that character is the antagonist.

Realism   Literature that seeks to present life as it is really lived by real people, without didacticism or moral agendas. In the eighteenth and nineteenth centuries realism was controversial; today it is usual.

Regionalism   Literature that is strongly identified with a specific place. Writers like Kate Chopin who concentrate on one area are called regional realists; writers who do so for several works are said to have strong regional elements in their body of work.

Rising action   The part of a story's action that develops its conflict and leads to its climax.

Setting   One of the elements of fiction, setting is the context for the action: the time, place, culture, and atmosphere in which it occurs. A work may have several settings; the relation among them may be significant to the meaning of the work.

Short story   A short work of narrative fiction whose plot, characters, settings, point of view, style, and theme reinforce each other, often in subtle ways, creating an overall unity.

Stream of consciousness   A narrative technique primarily based on the works of psychologist-philosophers Sigmund Freud, Henri Bergson, and William James, who originated the phrase in 1890. In fiction, the technique is designed to represent a character's inner thoughts, which flow in a stream without grammatical structure and punctuation or apparent coherence. The novels *Ulysses* and *Finnegans Wake*, by James Joyce, contain the most famous and celebrated use of the technique. Stream of consciousness, which represents the borders of consciousness, may be distinguished from the interior monologue, which is more structured and rational.

Structure   The organizational pattern or relation among the parts of a story. Questions to help determine a story's structure may include the following: Is the story told without stop from beginning to end, or is it divided into sections? Does the narrator begin at the beginning of a plot, or when actions are already under way (*in medias res*, in the middle of things)? Does the narrator begin at the end of the plot and tell the story through a series of flashbacks? Is the story organized by major events or episodes, or by images or moods?

Style One of the elements of fiction, style in a literary work refers to the diction (choice of words), syntax (arrangement of words), and other linguistic features of a work. Just as no two people have identical fingerprints or voices, so no two writers use words in exactly the same way. Style distinguishes one writer's language from another's.

Symbol A reference to a concrete image, object, character, pattern, or action whose associations evoke significant meanings beyond the literal ones. An archetype, or archetypal symbol, is a symbol whose associations are said to be universal—that is, they extend beyond the locale of a particular nation or culture. Religious symbols, such as the cross, are of this kind. In literature, *symbolism* refers to an author's use of symbols.

Theme One of the elements of fiction, the theme is the main idea that is explored in a story. Characters, plot, settings, point of view, and style all contribute to a theme's development.

Third-person narrator See **point of view.**

Tone Like tone of voice. Literary tone is determined by the attitude of a narrator toward characters in a story and the story's readers. For example, the tone of a work may be impassioned, playful, haughty, grim, or matter-of-fact. Tone is distinct from atmosphere, which refers to the mood of a story and can be analyzed as part of its setting.

Unity The oneness of a short story. Generally, each of a story's elements has a unity of its own, and all reinforce each other to create an overall unity. Although a story's unity may be evident on first reading, much more often discovering the unity requires rereading, reflection, and analysis. Readers who engage themselves in these ways experience the pleasure of bringing a story to life.

About the Editor

Pattie Cowell teaches American literature at Colorado State University, where she is a professor of English and a University Distinguished Teaching Scholar. While her major research has been in early American studies, she has also published articles on Herman Melville, B. Traven, Leslie Silko, multiculturalism, gothic fiction, service learning, and feminist pedagogy. In addition to extensive work on early American women poets culminating in *Women Poets in Pre-Revolutionary America* and *Critical Essays on Anne Bradstreet*, she has written on Cotton Mather, on the eighteenth-century magazine trade, and on the English letter writer Polly Hewson. Her work has appeared in such journals as *Early American Literature*, *Legacy*, *Signs*, and *American Literary History*, and in collections such as *Teaching the Literatures of Early America* (MLA) and *Finding Colonial Americas*

(University of Delaware Press). Serving many years as the early American field editor for the United States Authors Series (Twayne/G. K. Hall), she arranged for publication of Patricia L. Parker's volume on Susanna Rowson. A personal essay, "Deep Focus," appeared in *Prairie Schooner.* She is presently working on a series of essays about storytelling in the northern plains areas of Alberta, Saskatchewan, Montana, and the Dakotas.